BLOW THE SILVER TRUMPETS

Sermons for Pentecost [First Third]
Cycle C Gospel Texts
BY LARRY POWELL

C.S.S Publishing Co., Inc.
Lima, Ohio

BLOW THE SILVER TRUMPETS

Library of Congress Cataloging-in-Publication Data

Powell, Larry D., 1939-
   Blow the silver trumpets : sermons for Pentecost (first third),
Cycle C Gospel texts / by Larry Powell.
     p.   cm.
   ISBN 1-55673-314-3
   I. Pentecost—Sermons.   2. Pentecost season—Sermons.   3. Bible.
N.T. Gospels—Sermons.   4. Sermons, American.   I. Title.
BV4300.5.P68   1991
252'.6—dc20   91-2358
                                                 CIP

9135 / ISBN 1-55673-314-3   PRINTED IN U.S.A.

The Lord said to Moses, "Make two silver
trumpets; of hammered work you shall make
them; and you shall use them for summoning the congregation, and for breaking camp.
— Numbers 10:1, 2

Table Of Contents

Foreword   7

Pentecost   9
  Show Us The Father
  John 14:8-17; 25-27 [C]

Pentecost   21
  Are You Convinced
  John 15:26-27; 16:4b-11 [L]

Pentecost   33
  Receive The Holy Spirit
  John 20:19-23 [RC]

The Holy Trinity   45
  A Continuing Presence
  John 16:12-15

Proper 4   53
Pentecost 2
Ordinary Time 9
  Just Speak The Word
  Luke 7:1-10

Corpus Christi   63
  So Close . . . But Yet So Far
  Luke 9:11-17 [RC]

Proper 5   73
Pentecost 3
Ordinary Time 10
  But God Can
  Luke 7:11-17

Proper 6   83
Pentecost 4
Ordinary Time 11
      Tears And Ointment
      Luke 7:36-50

Proper 7   95
Pentecost 5
Ordinary Time 12
      To Be Or Not To Be . . . Is Not The Question
      Luke 9:18-24

Proper 8   105
Pentecost 6
Ordinary Time 13
      The Set Face And The Turned Head
      Luke 9:51-62

Proper 9   113
Pentecost 7
Ordinary Time 14
      Fleshing Out The Word
      Luke 10:1-12

Lectionary Preaching After Pentecost   122

C — Common Lectionary (Proper)
L — Lutheran Lectionary (Pentecost)
RC — Roman Catholic Lectionary (Ordinary Time)

Foreword

Surprised? You've discovered a lectionary library book that grabs your attention by the scruff of the neck and pulls you on page after page. What is the power of the pull? The illustrations? The insights? The biblical allusions?

Larry Powell breathes life into Scripture with a preacher's imagination, a poet's turn of the phrase, and a writer's craftsmanship. He gathers vibrant illustrations from everywhere. One moment you may be playing football or golf, or listening to a boxer, the the next moment you may be driving down an Arkansas road, looking at road signs or passing vans.

Saints and scholars, classical and friendly faces, each make their contribution. A timely quote from Euripides or Elton Trueblood, from Nietzsche or Ruth Graham, dot the literary landscape. As Jesus suggested, Larry Powell is like the merchant who gathers "something old, something new." Or like the bride, "something borrowed, something blue." Illustrations come from everywhere. Some are earthy, down home, personal.

You will remember walking with Larry and his wife to the "pump" in Tuscumbia, Alabama, where Helen Keller drank water, put her hand on her teacher's mouth, and "hearing" her first word, "water." You will never forget ambling into an old "junktique" store crammed from floor to ceiling with interesting old items, watching the proprietor pick his teeth, refusing to sell any of his wares because he enjoys them.

Some of us string illustrations along like putting beads on a thread. Larry Powell selects an illustration that is just right, the way a stone mason picks just the proper rock for the fireplace. Then Powell lets that illustration tell its story, fully and to the point.

Even though this volume is focused on New Testament passages, Old Testament characters jump into the narrative. Old friends, David and his slingshot, Gideon and his 300 man army,

King Nebuchadnezzar and his dream, 90-year-old Sarah, Moses and his sheep, help illuminate the spiritual realities of the New Testament story.

Hymn writers give their life testimony even as they pen their verse. You will again be inspired by Charles A. Tindley's "Stand By Me" and William Cowper's "God Moves In a Mysterious Way."

One of the writer's great gifts is his ability to nail down an idea or scriptural truth with a clinching biblical text or verse or poem.

Something deeper, though, is needed in a good lectionary book. We crave insight into God's Word, thoughtful inspection of the text, careful exploration of the ideas hinted at. Powell provides just that.

When the centurion, through his Jewish emissary, tells Jesus "Only say the word," Powell lifts up words that help and heal — words of reconciliation, words which remove fear (remember walking home as a child at night all alone, sidestepping "grotesque, stoop-shouldered, long fingered ogres who prey upon little children"), words which remove loneliness, words which heal, words of witness.

Preachers, not just lectionary preachers, need this book to help them preach. Teachers of Holy Scripture need it to help them teach. But all of us will profit by it on our bedside table or with us in an airplane. Broken down into bite size pieces, it is wonderful reading in a world of interruptions and short time frames. It provides spiritual inspiration and enjoyment.

Now, the last word of encouragement. Most lectionary books are jumpy, compartmentalized, cut up into parts, almost by necessity. Larry Powell's turn of a phrase; his sly sense of humor that makes you grin then look around to see if anyone is watching; and his pace, that is, his sense of intellectual progress, makes the book a unity. You literally can sit down and read it, cover to cover, and say, "That was a good book, an enjoyable book, a helpful book."

You will find yourself quoting from it as you visit with your friends or speak in the church. You just won't be able to help it.

But most of all, as you ponder these pages, you will look at Jesus Christ. You will listen to him, meditate on his message, watch him in action. You will be drawn to him in faith and trust, looking to him as Savior and leaning on him as Lord. For that is what Larry Powell's helpful book is all about.

Bishop Richard B. Wilke
The United Methodist Church
The Arkansas Area
July 20, 1990

Show Us The Father

A tourist stood for long periods of time upon the beach, facing away from the ocean, pressing a seashell against his ear. The water lapped at his feet, the sun beamed down upon his head and shoulders, and the waves crashed just behind him. Firmly, he pressed the seashell against his ear. He wanted to hear the powerful surge of the ocean as it heaved and rolled. See the picture in your mind's eye: a man standing with his back to the ocean, attempting to hear the ocean in a seashell. Although in the presence of the very thing he was seeking, he was oblivious to the actuality.

Some people have difficulty in recognizing that they have caught up to what they have been chasing, or are in the presence of the object of their desire. Such persons, in their extreme forms, are always running but never arriving, always searching but never discovering, always looking but never seeing, always measuring but the numbers are forever wrong. It would be unfair to describe Phillip and the other disciples as fitting this description, but then it would be equally unfair to suggest that they were incapable of obliviousness, particularly since our text begins, "Lord, show us the Father, and we shall be satisfied." Phillip and the others are reminiscent of the man standing by the sea listening for the sound of the ocean in a seashell.

Jesus and the 12 were in the upper room. The Passover meal had been shared, Jesus had washed the disciples' feet, and Judas had taken his leave. All things having been accomplished, Jesus informs the 11 that the time has come for his departure. Very brief dialogues with Simon Peter and Thomas follow, to which Jesus adds, "No one comes to the Father, but by me. If you had known me, you would have known my

11

Father also; henceforth you know him and have seen him (14:6-7).'' Let us underscore the part which reads, "If you had known me, you would have known my Father also.'' Apparently Phillip and the others did not hear that part, for no sooner had James gotten the words out of his mouth than Phillip asked, "Lord, show us the Father, and we will be satisfied.'' They had not been listening.

> *"Jesus said to him, 'Have I been with you so long, and yet you do not know me, Phillip? He who has seen me has seen the Father; how can you say, 'Show us the Father'? Do you not believe that I am in the Father and the Father in me? The words that I say to you I do not speak on my own authority; but the Father who dwells in me does his works (14:9-11)."*

Jesus knew that they had not been listening. He knew there had been numerous things said and done during the past three years which they had not gathered in.

I. The Request

"Show us the Father, and we shall be satisfied.'' Yes, we have heard that before. The Scriptures are replete with instances where the matter of God's visible presence is raised in one form or another. The Israelites in Egypt wanted to see God. They were familiar with poems and ancient stories about floods and rainbows. They wanted to see God. They knew all about handwriting on the wall, covenants, and Jacob's wrestling with an angel. But where was God when Egyptian taskmasters cracked their whips across the bleeding backs of God's chosen people? Chosen? For what? To make bricks? Don't talk to them about poems and old stories. Those things were no longer spiritually satisfying, "Show us the Father, and we will be satisfied.'' The Psalmist would one day make the same request: "Why does thou stand afar off, O Lord? Why does thou hide thyself in times of trouble (Psalm 10:1)?" Job said, "Oh, that I knew where I might find him, that I might come even to his seat (Job 23:3)." He wanted to see God. For centuries, the people of God had been braced up spiritually by the knowledge of burning bushes, the sun standing still, water from a rock, manna from the sky, and fiery, cloudy pillars. Those things were all good. But at times, recollections wear thin, especially when they are several generations old. Evidences of God are strong potions but there comes a time when a person wants something more than recollections and convictions. "Show us the Father, and we shall be satisfied," is not an unfamiliar request.

(1) Where is God when we experience reverses in our lives? Dr. Leslie Weatherhead recalled a story related to one of the vicious air raids over London during World War II. A father and mother were seated with their two children on the front porch enjoying the twilight. Suddenly, the sirens around the city began to sound in that frightening shrill, loud alarm. The Luftwaffe was approaching. The father and son hurried to a bomb shelter. In haste and confusion, the mother and daughter ran in another direction. The bombing was intense, savagely blasting away buildings, homes, and human lives. After what seemed like hours, the bombing ceased and the Luftwaffe disappeared into the smoke and clouds. In a while, the all-clear signal sounded and people cautiously emerged from wherever they had sought refuge. The father and son immediately set about to look for their loved ones, only to discover their lifeless bodies near the shattered debris which had once been their home. The father slumped to sit upon the ground. The son wandered into what had been the garden area. The sky was almost dark now and the stars were beginning to shine. Momentarily, the father called to the boy, "What are you doing, son?" With his eyes fixed upon the sky, the boy answered, "I'm watching God hang out the stars."

"Show us the Father" when devastating reverses occur in life. People want to know whether or not God presides over such things, allows such things, has anything to do with such things, or if there is a God at all! What a solace it is for the believer who, having already experienced a personal relationship with the Father, has resolved such questions before reverses occur. The knowledge of the presence of God thus becomes a strength to draw upon in times of crisis, rather than something to ponder and seek. The little British boy knew enough about God to know that whatever happened, however devastating, God would hang out the stars. If God can hang out the stars across the vast reaches of the heavens to illumine the darkness above us, of a truth, he is capable of dispelling the darkness within us.

(2) Where is God when evil is more evident than good? "Show us the Father" when evil is appearing to have its way. The July, 1990, issue of *Time* magazine reported that at least 600,000 Americans are infected with the AIDS virus, more than 136,000 have become sick, and some 83,000 of those have died. Victims of the disease basically fall into two categories: people who have had sex with infected individuals and drug addicts who acquired the virus from contaminated needles, which brings another monumental dilemma into the picture — drug abuse. There is no need to go into detail about the nature and extent of crime problems directly related to drug addiction. Moreover, there is no need to dwell here upon identifying evil in its many forms in order to establish that there are times when evil appears to be more evident than the good. What we really want to know is, "Where is God when evil has its way?" and the ache deep down in our souls causes us to cry out, "Show us the Father." Christian friend, it is all in knowing how to look. Many of you will remember that several years ago one of the Russian cosmonauts left his capsule and floated in space, remarking to the mission control that he did not "see" God anywhere. C. S. Lewis has said, "If a man never sees God on the earth, he will never see him in space; but if a man sees God here in the faces of men and women in his daily life, then when you hurl him into space, he will put his hand upon the face of God." Lewis concludes, "The seeing eye is tremendously important." The eye discerns such evidence as it is equipped to acknowledge.

(3) Where is God when death reaches into our circle? A friend of mine from seminary days at Candler School of Theology in Atlanta commuted on weekends to his pastorate in Alabama. He was extremely likeable, held in high regard by his fellow seminarians, and thoroughly committed to serving God through the pastoral ministry. On a particular Monday, he did not return to school. Tuesday, there were two or three passing inquiries concerning his whereabouts. By Wednesday, some of us were wondering if perhaps he was ill. Thursday, my friend returned to school. He shared with me that his wife had died on Saturday and was buried on Monday. Hindered throughout her life by an asthmatic condition, she was fatally overcome by steam while taking a shower. Yes, she had taken many showers throughout her life. What was different about this one? He did not know. Those kind of puzzling questions only serve to make tragedies more difficult. Tuesday and Wednesday, he had personal affairs to tend. Thursday, he was back in school. "I just got to thinking," he said, "about all the times someone has said to me, 'Where was God when my son died?' and I have given them the standard preacher-answer, 'He was in the same place, doing the same thing he was when his son died.' My wife was God's daughter and I am God's son and if the answer I've been giving people is worth anything, it ought to be worth something to me. I know God is grieved. I know too, with Paul, that I am able to do all things through Christ who strengthens me. So, the best thing I can do is take up here where God wants me to be, where my wife would want me to be, and where I need to be."

"Show us the Father," my friend could have cried out in remorse. But he already knew the whereabouts of the Father.

"Show us the Father, and we shall be satisfied," Phillip asked on behalf of the others. We know all about that kind of request, especially when we experience reverses in our lives, when evil appears to have its way, and when death reaches into our circle of family and friends.

15

II. The Reply

Have you ever received an answer in reply which left you feeling incredibly dumb? Recently, my wife and I were driving in the Lakewood area of North Little Rock in search of a rather famous landmark known as the "Old Mill." Apparently, everybody in the state of Arkansas has visited the place because it seems to come up in most every conversation. We had heard about its being included in the movie, "Gone With The Wind," how it is a popular site for weddings, and what a work of art it is. It was time for us to go see it. For 10 or 15 minutes we drove around the Lakewood area. You know how men are when driving in a strange place, insisting that if you drive around long enough, you will eventually find what you are looking for. Having been made to feel stupid so many times for doing that very thing, I reasoned after 10 or 15 minutes to stop the car and ask the first person who gave the appearance of knowing where we wanted to go. A man and woman were walking briskly along the sidewalk. "Pardon me," I said, "could you tell us how to get to the Old Mill?" He pointed to his right. "See that sign right there that says Old Mill?" he asked. The sign was in clear view. I wished I had not asked. I felt, well, stupid, which was what I was trying to avoid feeling in the first place. The "Are-you-blind-fellow?" expression on the man's face didn't do a great deal to remove any of the sting from the moment.

Jesus did not say it this way, but it may have seemed so, "Are you blind, Phillip? Have I been with you for so long and you still do not recognize me? He who has seen me has seen the Father; how can you say, 'Show us the Father'?" We have the strong suspicion that Phillip wished he had not made the request.

Jesus replied that "He who hath seen me hath seen the Father." We will not dwell on that. Surely, enough has been said about the Word becoming flesh, God emptying himself in Christ, and resulting Christologies that it is unnecessary to elaborate upon this part of Jesus' reply at the expense of at least two other things which are eternally important.

(1) Another counselor. Jesus was referring now to something else which Phillip and the others could not gather in. How it must have seemed to them that he was given to speaking in peculiar, coined-for-the-occasion phrases. There had been so many phrases turned in novel ways. Nicodemus, the Pharisee, had come to Jesus one night and declared that only the power of God could explain the signs and wonders which Jesus performed. Jesus replied, "Truly, truly, I say to you, unless one is born anew, he cannot see the kingdom of God (John 3:3)." That reply required some explanation. Later, Jesus would speak to the disciples about there being many rooms in his Father's house and that he was going to prepare the way for them to follow. He said confidently, "And you know the way where I am going (John 14:f)." It was then that Thomas spoke up and said, "Lord, we don't even know where you are going; how can we know the way?" Jesus said something else about the way, the truth, and the life, and then mentioned something about knowing him and knowing God. Phillip was then heard to say, "Lord, show us the Father, and we shall be satisfied." There had been all of that, and more, and now comes this talk about another "Counselor."

The Holy Spirit. That is what Jesus was talking about. We have such an advantage of perspective which the disciples did not have. We have everything the Bible says about the Spirit, plus what the church and theologians say about the Spirit, plus what we know and have experienced personally. And yet, at best, it seems we can only speak in similes. In *The Wind and the Spirit*, Vance Havner refers to Jesus' comment that the Spirit is like the wind: "There is mystery, there is power, and we cannot chart the course of the Spirit. He is sovereign to do as he pleases, just as the wind blows where it lists." Havner then explains, "He did not use the same method or manner with Savonarola and Knox and Luther and Wesley and Moody. Just as there are hurricanes and zephyrs, so the Spirit storms and soothes. He speaks in mighty tornado or gentlest whisper. The Spirit did not work in the Reformation as he did in the Great Awakening." Nor was the Great Awakening the same

17

as the Welsh Revival. And the manner in which the Spirit worked in the Welsh Revival was not the same as your personal experience of the Spirit. And your personal experience was different than anyone else's you know. The Spirit — counselor, adviser, companion, teacher — is like the wind, blowing as it listeth.''

(2) Be not troubled nor be afraid. Jesus promised to bestow a blessed "peace" upon his followers. There is, after all, a peace in "knowing," isn't there? The security of knowing that God is in control, a Counselor is ever near, and in ways which we cannot imagine, the Spirit is leading. Worry and fear are an insult to the Spirit because they indicate a certain lack of confidence in what the Spirit is designed to do in the first place. Worry and fear then, are sure evidence that the presence of the Holy Spirit is being ignored and the power of the Holy Spirit is being discounted. To reject the presence and power of the Spirit is to reject the peace which our Lord has promised to bestow.

The presence and power of the Spirit enable things of the kingdom to be accomplished despite our troubled and worried attitudes. It is told that Newman Hall stood early one morning on the summit of Snowden in Wales, accompanied by approximately 120 others. They had all climbed to this high vantage point to behold what they had hoped to be a breathtaking sunrise. They were not disappointed. The sunlight bathed the mountain peaks and danced upon scattered lakes in the valley below. It was a special moment. Someone invited Dr. Hall to preach. Himself, overcome by the wonder of the experience, Dr. Hall realized that he was too emotional to preach. Instead, he knelt and began praying aloud. As he reached deep within his soul and attempted to put into words the kind of things which are difficult to put into words, tears filled his eyes. With heads bowed and eyes closed, the people were riveted to the sound of his voice. In a while, and in a strange attitude of awe, everyone descended the mountain and went their own way. Dr. Hall would learn sometime later that 40 people had been converted that morning and joined the church.

"That is strange," he said, "I did not say anything directly to them; I only prayed." He was then informed, "Yes, and what is even more wonderful is they did not know a word you said, for none of them speak English, only Welsh."

The Spirit blows where it wills. The promised Counselor is present as advisor, companion, and teacher. The Holy Spirit is the agent of peace, accomplishing its work despite our lack of confidence and limited understanding.

"Show us the Father," you say. Christian friend, do not be like the man standing in the presence of the sea, listening for its sound in a seashell. You are in the presence of the Father, Son, and Holy Spirit now. Do not turn your back upon the actuality of your soul's desire, the actuality of our peace.

Are You Convinced?

Someone has astutely observed that our culture does not handle "endings" very well. "Beginnings," on the other hand, seem to come off quite nicely. Weddings, beautiful and memorable in themselves, are also occasions for parties, bridal showers, gift bearing, and other happy kinds of experiences which we usually associate with the celebration of two persons in love beginning a new home. When a home is blessed with a newborn, balloons, flowers, photographs, gifts, a host of well-wishes, and perhaps even a sign in the yard, are common place. When a new business is opened, there is a house warming. When a new ship is christened, a bottle of champagne is smashed against it. When a new product is made available, consumers are pumped up about it long before it even hits the shelf and, ordinarily, the debut of the new product inspires a once-in-a-lifetime sale designed as an added incentive to attract customers. The inauguration of a new president of the United States, the swearing-in of elected officials, and the ordination and consecration of persons into religious offices — all these, and more, are familiar reminders of how we have dignified and formalized "beginnings." This is not to suggest that all beginnings inspire elation or create fond memories. It is to suggest that "beginnings" are considerably more ritualized than "endings."

Student Pastor

As a student pastor, I served a three-point charge. The first few days in the new pastorate resembled the ritual commonly observed by a new pastor and his flock as they introduce themselves and "size each other up." This particular parish had historically been served by young pastors pursuing a college education. The parishioners had made their peace with the fact that as soon as one pastor would complete educational requirements and graduate, a new student pastor would appear on the scene. It was my second day on the job. I walked up and down the streets meeting everybody in sight, determined that my ministry in that place was going to count for something. Stopping at a home I knew to belong to church members, I was invited in to sit on the front porch. The man and his wife sat in a wooden swing which creaked slightly as it moved lazily back and forth. The usual pleasantries were exchanged, topics for discussion were awkwardly reached for, and the obligatory questions asked. Feeling confident that I had made a reasonably good first impression, I dismissed myself, opened the screen door, and stepped into the yard. As I left, the woman whispered, or tried to whisper to the man, "Same old thing, same old thing." Not all beginnings are knee-slapping, high-water mark, ecstatic experiences. Beginnings are, however, acknowledged by at least some semblance of formality.

On the other hand, we do not make much of "finalities." When a building has served its purpose, a wrecking-ball or bulldozer will level it to the ground without benefit of a ribbon cutting, speeches, or assembled guests. When a marriage is dissolved, it usually is not a graceful thing to behold and rather than the community being involved in its proceedings, the community usually makes an effort to stay as far removed from it as possible. There are so many terminations and finalities about which we seem to do so very little. And then, there is the final termination — death. Even with the best of intentions, we tend to fumble awkwardly in the presence of death, wanting to say the proper thing, do the proper thing, allow the proper thing. Endings are handled differently than beginnings, aren't they? Beginnings seem to be so much easier. Endings, should we allow ourselves to become involved in them, would appear to require so much more from us. And then, there is the threat that we could become a part of the finality itself, or part of the perpetuation. There is a genuine risk involved with being actually involved with an ending, you see. Apparently, the disciples were uncertain as to which alternative reality was immediately thrusting upon them.

There is no mistaking that our text portrays Jesus preparing his disciples for a termination, a ministry of presence and power, rapidly ending:

> *"I did not say these things to you from the beginning, because I was with you. But now I am going to him who sent me (16:5)."*

Jesus, knowing the time was at hand, was desperately attempting to provide some explanation about what was happening, and why. Who could possibly have missed his meaning? However, please observe that from this point on, the disciples did not handle the "ending" very well. Judas and a band of soldiers stormed the garden where Jesus and the others had gathered. Judas carried his money bag; the soldiers carried "lanterns, torches, and weapons." Judas botched the ending badly. Simon Peter grabbed up a sword and took a reckless swipe at one of the soldiers, Malchus, cutting off his ear. Jesus then reminded Peter that he had only moments before explained the present distress:

> *"It is to your advantage that I go away, for if I do not go away, the Counselor will not come to you (16:7)."*

Resistance, Jesus explained, was out of order. In a little while, Peter would be standing at a safe distance from where Jesus had been taken, warming himself by a fire, repeatedly denying that he had ever known Jesus. Simon Peter botched the ending in the most miserable manner. The other disciples were equally as disappointing: afraid, hiding, trying to figure out some way to get back to the way of life they had known be-fore they had followed the carpenter. What is so hauntingly conspicuous is the fact that nowhere do we read that any of those to whom Jesus spoke in our text, understood, tried to understand, nor even remembered anything he had said. Had they understood at the time, or even sorted the meaning later, there would have been no betrayals, denials, or plans to go back to old professions.

Being A Witness

So much for terminations. Sometimes we don't handle be-ginnings very well either. The disciples didn't. Jesus had spoke to them about the importance of their being witnesses to him in the future, beginning at that moment, even more loyally than they had before. They did not get that part. The really wonderful thing which was to soon begin, however, was that the new Counselor would come to convince the world:

> *"concerning sin, because they do not believe in me; con-cerning righteousness, because I go to the Father, and you will see me no more; concerning judgment, because the ruler of this world is judged (vv. 9-11)."*

They did not get that part either. But, in all fairness, let us admit that the parts are not always easy to gather in. The dis-ciples were being challenged to understand a revolutionary thought in an exceedingly brief amount of time. The world has now had 2,000 years to digest the same thought. We have managed to get it down on paper well enough and have found it to be logically feasible. The difficulty arises when we come to the matter of practical application. For some reason or another, the way of Christ and the leadership of the Holy Spirit are easier to talk about than to bear witness to. Let us think specifically now about the business of the Christian as a wit-ness, in conjunction with the witness of the Spirit.

"You are my witnesses" (v. 27). Jesus was declaring that the great work of the kingdom was not something which had been designed for him to accomplish alone. Had such been the case, there would have been no need to enlist the 12 in the first place. Had such been the case, Christianity would be a "do nothing" religion, requiring nothing more than personal assent.

A No-hitter

Andy Hawkins, pitcher for the New York Yankees, will go down in baseball history for pitching a no-hitter on July 1, 1990. Little boys dream of going to the big leagues and becoming star athletes by excelling at their position. Can you imagine how many major league pitchers have come and gone without ever pitching a no-hitter? Scores of them never came close. No-hitters are extra-special, an achievement amounting to a dream performance by a champion athlete. Why then was the no-hitter against the Chicago White Sox a bittersweet experience for Andy Hawkins? Because he lost. That's right, he lost. How does a pitcher lose a no-hitter. Because his teammates committed three errors on routine plays in the eighth inning. Hawkins had done his best, had not allowed a hit, and had accomplished all that he had been asked to do. He was depending upon his teammates just as they were counting on him. On that day, he was a winner, but his teammates dropped the ball. We would not be so foolish as to substitute any of this as being analogous to Jesus, the disciples, the Holy Spirit, or the Christian witness. We will suggest, however, that Jesus Christ has already accomplished all that the Father had asked him to do and it is certainly within our prerogative to botch the role that the Holy Spirit seeks to inspire within each of us, because of tentativeness or missed opportunities. Again, Jesus declared his dependence upon and confidence in those who would be witnesses because the great work of the kingdom was not something which had been designed for him to accomplish alone.

"Concerning sin (v. 9)." The Holy Spirit will convince the world concerning sin. The late Dr. J. Wilbur Chapman told of a preacher who frequently preached about sin. The preacher, although a man of tact, did not mince words when he warmed to his subject. "Sin," he insisted, "is that abominable thing that God hates." There would be no mistaking the burden he carried on his heart for the redemption of sinners. Once, a leading layperson in his congregation came to him and requested that he refrain from using the word "sin." The layperson reasoned, "We wish you would not speak so plainly about sin. Our youth and children hearing you will be more than likely to indulge in sin if you keep referring to it. Call it something else, such as inhibition, or error, or mistake, or even a twist in our nature. It would just be better if you would quit using the word sin." The preacher replied, "I know what you mean." He then walked deliberately to his desk and brought out a little bottle. "This bottle," he said, "contains strychnine. You will notice that the red label on the bottle reads, 'poison.' Would you suggest that I remove this label and replace it with another which reads, 'Wintergreen'?" He then added, "The more harmless the name, the more dangerous the dose will become."

Call Sin By Its Name

If the Holy Spirit, through Christians as witnesses, is going to convince anyone about sin, one of the first things we are going to have to do is call sin by its name: sin. Dr. Karl Menninger, the famous psychiatrist, assures us that "sin" really does exist. He has expressed his personal distress that modern society attempts to resolve its problems and prattle on about morality without ever mentioning the word, "sin." A publication called, *Pastor's Manual*, reports that Dr. Menninger is "convinced that the only way to raise the moral tone of present-day civilization and deal with the depression and worries that plague clergy, psychiatrists, and ordinary folk is to revive an understanding of what 'sin' is.'' We are convinced that Dr. Menninger is correct and we are convinced that it will be through Christian witnesses declaring Christ that the Holy Spirit will convince the world concerning sin.

Let us pray that the Holy Spirit will convince us that the sinner is not always the other fellow. D. L. Moody was invited to preach once in a church where some of the members were accustomed to leaving before the sermon ended. The minister of the church forewarned the evangelist about the custom, then apologized for those who were certain to leave early that morning. When Mr. Moody entered the pulpit, he boldly announced, ''I am going to speak to two classes of people this morning: first to the sinners, and then to the saints.'' He proceeded to address the sinners for a time and then announced, ''The sinners may now leave.'' It is reported that, for once, all members of the congregation remained until the sermon had ended and even lingered following the benediction.

The Holy Spirit will convince the world concerning sin when we become convinced that the great work of the kingdom is not something which was designed for the Holy Spirit to do alone. We have already referred to Dr. J. Wilbur Chapman who, in addition to telling about the preacher who spoke plainly about sin, has made an interesting observation about the New Testament. He has determined that the New Testament tells of 40 people, each suffering from the same disease, who were healed by Jesus. Thirty-four were either brought to Jesus by friends, or he was taken to them. In only six cases of the 40 did the afflicted come to Jesus without assistance. The conclusion? ''Of the vast number of people who find their way to Jesus today, most of them reach him because the friends of Jesus are concerned about the welfare of their souls.''

''Concerning righteousness (v. 10).'' We are speaking now of persons who dwell in the ''way of right,'' or have been ''put right.'' The word, and especially the concept, is potentially offensive to persons who are uncomfortable about being around another who may have reason to be condescending. Clarence Mecartney tells that Aristides the Just was present at the Athenian assembly when that body voted that he should be banished. A member from the country, illiterate and not knowing who Aristides was, wished to vote for his banishment. As it happened, he went up to Aristides and asked him to please write the name "Aristides" on a shell for him to signify his vote for exile. As Aristides wrote his name on the shell, he asked the man, "Do you know Aristides or have anything against him?" The man replied, "No, I do not know him nor do I hold anything against him. I just get tired of hearing him spoken of as Aristides the Just." Likewise, there are some who may attach certain negative connotations to the word, "righteousness," or to such a person who may be referred to as righteous. That does not matter. The Scriptures are plain:

> *"The times of ignorance God overlooked, but now he commands all men everywhere to repent because he has fixed a day on which he shall judge the world in righteousness by a man whom he has appointed (Acts 17:30-31)."*

The world will be judged in righteousness and there is help for those who seek after righteousness:

> *"All Scripture is inspired by God and profitable for teaching, for reproof, for correction, and for training in righteousness, that the man of God may be complete, equipped for every good work (2 Timothy 3:16-17)."*

The Last Judgment will be done in righteousness:

> *"Then I saw heaven opened, and beheld, a white horse! He who sat upon it is called Faithful and True, and in righteousness he judges (Revelation 19:11)."*

And what of the righteous on the Judgment Day?

"Henceforth there is laid up for me the crown of right-eousness, which the Lord, the righteous judge, will award to me on that Day, and not to me only, but also to all who have loved his appearing (2 Timothy 4:8)."

We are convinced that righteousness is the way of the Lord, that which we should seek after, is the promised reward to all those who persevere, and confirmed by the Holy Spirit to others by and through Christian witnesses.

Secret Of Patience

Dr. J. Kenneth Shamblin, in his book, *Life Comes As Choice*, tells about one of his dear friends, a skilled doctor, who poured out his life for other people in such an unselfish manner that Dr. Shamblin admired him greatly. One day, he said to the doctor, "I would like to know the secret of your patience and how it is that you have so much understanding for the burdens people carry. You never seem to quit a person because they do not strive to live to the best they could be. You seem to especially stand by those who are weak in body and spirit who could be doing better." The doctor replied: "Kenneth, I'll have to tell you how much I've been forgiven. If you know what the grace of God had done in my own life, then you could understand why I am able to mean a little bit to many people." Shamblin concluded from that conversation that "every person who ever lived stands in the presence of both guilt and grace, and we have to choose which one we want to use and live with. One means ruin and disaster; the other means a new morning, a new task, a new ability, a new gift from God." Every person makes this choice.

The Holy Spirit will convince the world of righteousness when we become convinced that the great work of the kingdom is not something which is designed for the Holy Spirit to do alone.

"Concerning judgment (v. 11)." Christians have long professed to believe in a day of accountability. Such a day is not marked on the calendar nor even claimed to occur in proximity to some speculated date. All the more reason to be ready for the event whenever it should occur. All the more reason to, as the saints of yesteryear put it, "warn others of the wrath to come." Someone has told that the thing which made William Booth a radical Salvationist was the accusing, mocking statement of an infidel who proclaimed in a lecture, "If I believed what you Christians say you believe with reference to the coming judgment and day of reckoning, with the result being eternal lostness of those who reject your Christ, then I would crawl on my bare knees on crushed glass all over London, England, night and day, telling people to flee from the wrath to come." The obvious implication being that Christians do not give the appearance of being convinced that judgment will actually come. What is your own personal witness in regard to the matter? Is there such about your life that evidences a consciousness of judgment? If the ministry of the Holy Spirit is to convict and convince persons of the judgment, it must have the cooperation and witness of those who profess to already be convicted and convinced.

A young lawyer in New York sat in his law office alone early one morning. Charles Finney was his name. The Holy Spirit began to deal with him in a strange and unmistakable way. Finney later described the experience as being an exchange between the Holy Spirit and his own soul which went:

"Finney, what are you going to do when you finish this course?"

"Put out a shingle and practice law."

"Then what?"

"Get rich."

"Then what?"

"Retire."

"Then what?"

"Die."

"Then what?"

"The judgment." At that, Finney ran into the woods and began praying, resolving not to leave until he had made his peace with God. In his mind, he saw himself before the judgment bar of God appearing as a vain, selfish hedonist. That evening he emerged from the woods a new person, going on to make his witness in life not as a lawyer but as a preacher, eventually bringing thousands to Christ over a 50-year ministry.

If the world is to be convinced of judgment, we must be convinced of judgment.

Jesus said the Holy Spirit will convince the world of sin, righteousness, and judgment! Are you convinced?

Because the Counselor, the Holy Spirit, has come, this moment can mark the end of an old way of life for you now if you will allow it. It can mark the beginning of a new way of life. Should we choose to do nothing, then we have botched both the beginning and the ending.

Receive The Holy Spirit

"It is my heart-warming and world-embracing hope," said Mark Twain, "that all of us — the high, the low, the rich, the poor, the admired, the despised, the loved, the hated, the civilized, and the savage — may eventually be gathered in a heaven of everlasting rest and peace and bliss, except the inventor of the telephone." Mark Twain obviously held a great dislike for the telephone, probably because, among other things, it renders a person to be easily accessible, even when they prefer to be inaccessible. Of course, someone is always quick to remind us, "You don't have to answer the telephone." We know that. But we also know, with Mark Twain, that the presence of the telephone effects an incredible impact upon our daily lives. Particularly now that mobile telephones and cordless models are so commonplace, the telephone suggests a kind of "ever-presence." Not only is it everywhere, but because of the rapid access it provides, we can be almost anywhere in seconds. To express it in a very unrefined manner, the telephone allows one's presence to be spread around and the very thought of that is not always exhilarating to someone who is not all that keen about anyone having easy access to their presence. Remember this the next time your telephone rings and you answer it to discover a voice on a computer inviting you to purchase siding for your home. Twain may have had a point.

We deal with all kinds of things which appear to be "ever-presences," don't we: responsibilities, concerns, medical conditions, financial obligations, never-ending drudgeries which are to do over and over, and so on. But what occupies a person and the extent to which it occupies them is not the same for everybody. What is considered "ever-present" in a person's life is largely determined by what one chooses to be ever-present.

There is another kind of Ever-Presence, so totally permeating all things, that it abides quite beyond the choice and preference of any of us. It just is and it, let us say, spreads its presence around:

> *"On the evening of that day, the first day of the week, the doors being shut where the disciples were, for fear of the Jews, Jesus came and stood among them and said to them, 'Peace be with you.' When he had said this, he showed them his hands and his side. Then the disciples were glad when they saw the Lord. Jesus said to them again, 'Peace be with you. As the Father has sent me, even so I send you.' And when he had said this, he breathed on them, and said to them, 'Receive the Holy Spirit. If you forgive the sins of any, they are forgiven; if you retain the sins of any, they are retained' (John 20:19-23)."*

> *"When the day of Pentecost had come, they were all together in one place. And suddenly a sound came from heaven like the rush of a mighty wind, and it filled all the house where they were sitting. And there appeared to them tongues as of fire, distributed and resting on each one of them. And they were all filled with the Holy Spirit . . . (Acts 2:1-3)."*

Moreover, the potential of the Holy Spirit is unlimited. According to Paul, the life which seeks only after things of this world achieves corruption and death, while life in the Spirit achieves eternal life (Galatians 6:8); the Holy Spirit intercedes for us with sighs too deep for words (Romans 8:26); participation in the Spirit is the common experience of all Christians (Philippians 2:1); the Holy Spirit unifies the church, enabling it to transcend worldly affairs (1 Corinthians 12:13); the Holy Spirit will transform the natural body into a spiritual body (2 Corinthians 5:5). There are some specific gifts, or fruits of the Spirit: "love, joy, peace, patience, kindness, goodness, faithfulness, gentleness and self-control (Galatians 5:22, 23)." What a remarkable "presence." Oh, we will not produce an exhaustive definition of the Holy Spirit and its work here; we can only refer to it in multiple ways. One might as well attempt to produce a photograph of the wind. It is possible to see where the wind is blowing, where it has been, and feel it upon our faces, but to actually see, or describe the wind, that is another matter. So it is with attempting to define the Holy Spirit. It is possible to see where it has been, and feel its presence upon our lives, but it is not within human capacity to satisfactorily describe nor explain exhaustively the Holy Spirit, commonly referred to in the New Testament by the word, "paraclete." Angus Benigus Sanrey, a French theologian, wrote a ponderous volume titled, *Paracletus seu de recta pronumciationa tractatus,* in the 17th century. The sole purpose of the work was to establish the correct pronunciation of one word, *Paracletus.* The Bible simply translates the word simply as Comforter. Ironically, neither the French theologian nor the word Comforter ever begin to gather the full meaning of the word *Paraclete* or the nature and function of the Counselor to whom Jesus referred. Christians, however, do not distress about not being able to construct a succinct, beautifully worded paragraph packaging the sum-total of the Third Person of the Trinity, form and function described in detail. The really distressing thing would be if it were limited to the extent that we could understand it.

It is significant, is it not, that following the resurrection when Jesus appeared to the disciples, showing them his hands and his side, he did not make any explanations. Twice he said, "Peace be with you." Twice he said, "Receive the Holy spirit." The words, "Peace be with you," were spoken as both a greeting and a blessing. The words, "Receive the Holy Spirit," contain something more: invitation, confirmation, and consecration.

1. Invitation: Jesus was inviting the disciples to acknowledge and receive the Holy Spirit — the divine Ever-Presence. Three years prior he had extended an invitation of a different nature, saying, "Follow me." The invitation was

such as would summon them from their fishing nets and tax tables; from their families, friends, and securities. To what?

> *"These 12 Jesus sent out, charging them, 'Go nowhere among the Gentiles, and enter no town of the Samaritans, but go rather to the lost sheep of the house of Israel. And preach as you go, saying, "The kingdom of heaven is at hand." Heal the sick, raise the dead, cleanse the lepers, cast out demons (Matthew 10:5-8).' "*

The initial invitation had involved commitment to the person of Christ and his ministry. As Lord of their lives, his ministry would be their ministry. But there was more:

> *"He who receives you receives me, and he who receives me receives him who sent me (Matthew 10:40)."*

Have you given serious consideration to the invitation which the minister extends near the end of a service of worship? In the minister's mind, it is the extension of an opportunity for someone outside of Christ to come forward and publicly embrace Jesus Christ as Lord. Whatever else we might say about this invitation is redundant unless one first embraces Jesus Christ as Lord. That is how the invitation is understood from the minister's perspective. What about from the laity's perspective? It may or may not be a case of being in concert. We have known for some time now throughout the church that we can no longer assume that everyone (even in the same congregation) is on the same wavelength. In fact, any assumption about doctrine, interpretation of Scripture, attitude toward mission, or most anything else, is clearly inappropriate. Is everyone even reasonably in agreement then regarding the invitation? This concern was brought into clearer focus for me once because of a remark made by a very keen-minded associate minister. We had both spoken before about the possibility of not standing in the narthex following morning worship to greet people because whatever door we would stand by, it seemed 90 percent of the people would exit by another door.

People were obviously in a hurry to get off the premises, beat worshipers from other churches to the cafeteria, eat lunch and be on their way for whatever the rest of the day might hold in store. The associate minister and I alternated standing at the various doors but there were just too many doors. One morning, we were discussing a new family in the community with whom we had visited and knew to be interested in transferring their membership to our congregation. I remarked to the associate, "Now if they come forward this morning, after we have received them into membership, you will want to accompany them to the narthex and I will invite everyone to welcome them." The associate said, "Following the benediction, I will just whisper to the new family, 'I invite you to join me in the narthex to be ignored'." We both smiled at each other about the prospect of such a thing, but as it turned out, it would have almost been appropriate. No more than a half-dozen people greeted the new family. Only moments before there had been well over 300 people in the sanctuary. I do not know how many other congregations are of the "get-out-of-my-way" mentality following worship on Sunday mornings, but there is at least one and when a new member or a new Christian is invited to the narthex to be welcomed, there is the real possibility that it could turn into an invitation to be "ignored." Please do not suggest that I proceed to chastise, shame, or even try to charm the congregation into a more congenial spirit. In the first place, I no longer pastor that congregation. In the second place, that "modus operandi" was attempted until it wore exceedingly thin. What is the invitation extended to new Christians or new members by your congregation? Is it an opportunity to celebrate with fellow Christians in the extension of the fellowship of Christ? Or, are these new friends in Christ invited to stand at the chancel or in the narthex and be largely ignored by a fellowship which has only moments before assumed certain responsibilities pertaining to their spiritual life? Invitations, like personal characters, come in different sizes.

Billy Sunday's music director, a Mr. Rodeheaver whose first name is not known to me, recorded the following story about a young boy who sang in his choir. The boy's name was Joey and Rodeheaver delicately noted that Joey was not "quite right." However, the lad would not leave the tabernacle at night until he had managed a hand shake from the music director. "It was sometimes embarrassing the way he would stand against me and wait until the last person had gone before he would say goodbye," Rodeheaver admitted. One evening a man came to speak to him and made it a point to thank him for being so kind to Joey. "He isn't quite right," the man said, "but he has never enjoyed anything so much as coming here and singing in the choir. He has worked hard through the day in order to be ready to come here at night, and it was because Joey invited my wife and our five children that we are here. Joey's 75-year-old grandfather and his dear wife are also here tonight and we want to do whatever is necessary to come to the Lord." People come in different sizes and so do invitations.

Jesus initially invited his disciples to receive him as Lord: "Follow me." Two thousand years later, this remains the initial step which we are invited to make. Then later, Jesus extended the invitation to the disciples to receive the Holy Spirit — "The Spirit of truth who proceeds from the Father," as he expressed it. Two invitations. The second being offered as the ever-present manifestation of the first; an invitation appropriately extended to all those of any age who confess Jesus Christ as Lord: "Receive the Holy Spirit."

2. Confirmation. Jesus made so many promises. For the most part, they were rather spectacular promises, weren't they? "Ask, and it will be given you; seek and you will find; knock and it will be opened to you. For everyone who asks receives, and he who seeks finds, and to him who knocks it shall be opened (Luke 11:9-11)." Sweeping words spoken privately to the disciples without any reservations whatsoever. "The Holy Spirit will teach you (in times of trouble) what you are to say (Luke 12:12);" "Fear not, little flock for it is your Father's good pleasure to give you the kingdom (Luke 12:32);" "Do you think that I have come to give peace on earth? No, I tell you, but rather division (Luke 12:51)." So many more. And

38

then there was all that business about the Son of Man being "mocked and scourged and crucified and raised on the third day (Matthew 20:19)." To name only these few, stop and consider what an incredibly mind-bending spectrum of remote possibilities Jesus was laying out before his disciples as absolute certainties. He was asking them to gather in a great many things for which they would have to stretch to reach. In time, however, they would slowly come to understand that if something had been promised, no matter how spectacular, it would be accomplished. Even the part about "the Counselor, the Holy Spirit, whom the Father will send in my name." One by one, the promises were confirmed. Take notice of that. See in your mind's eye Jesus standing in the Spirit before his disciples, showing them his hand and side confirming all that he had promised.

The post-resurrection appearance to the disciples confirmed some things, connected some things, which reached back considerably beyond the life and ministry of Jesus. (a) It confirmed the consistency of God's plan through the ages. In Old Testament times a great procession was conducted through the streets of Jerusalem on the last day of the feast of tabernacles. The procession moved slowly from the temple through the city streets, out the Water Gate, down the hill of Zion to the pool of Siloam. There, the white-robed priests who had marched at the front of the procession filled their golden vessels with water. The procession then retraced its steps to the temple where the priests gathered around the altar of sacrifice and emptied their vessels of water against the side of the altar. As the vessels were being emptied the Levitic choir chanted the words of Isaiah 12:3: "With joy shall you draw water out of the wells of salvation." The New Testament records that seven and a half centuries after Isaiah wrote these words, Jesus of Nazareth stood near the temple watching the traditional procession, listening to the music of the trumpets and the chanting of the Levites on the last great day of the feast of tabernacles. Above it all, the voice of Jesus was heard to proclaim, "If any man thirst, let him come unto me, and drink (John 7:37)."

We can almost hear the click of the link as it snaps into place, connecting God's great chain of redemptive events. But there is more:

> *"Now this he said about the Spirit, which those who be-lieved in him were to receive; for as yet the Spirit had not been given, because Jesus was not yet glorified. When they heard these words, some of the people said, 'This is really the prophet.' Others said, 'This is the Christ.' But some said, 'Is the Christ to come from Galilee? Has not the Scripture said that the Christ is descended from David, and comes from Bethlehem, the village where David was?' So there was division among the people over him. Some of them wanted to arrest him, but no one laid hands on him (John 7:39-44)."*

It does not matter that there was division over him. What was done, was done. Later, as Jesus appeared in the Spirit to the disciples, another link snapped into place, confirming the consistency of God's plan through the ages; (b) it confirmed the incalculable power of God. Someone has told that engineers in New York, years ago, sought a base for one of the buttresses of a bridge they were constructing. In the process, they happened upon an old scow full of bricks and heavy stones that had long ago sunk and remained almost totally buried in mud. Skilled, experienced divers were send down to place giant chains beneath the scow in order to raise it. Laboring with even such "modern" equipment as was available at the time, every effort failed. The heavy load could not be raised. Finally, one of the younger engineers declared that he was confident that the project could be accomplished if he be allowed to proceed. It was agreed that his plan would be allowed. He brought two barges to locate near the sunken scow. The huge chains were attached around the scow and secured to heavy beams on the barges. After tightening the chains at low tide, they waited. In time, the tide swept up the harbor in mighty heaves, raising the buried scow. It was raised by the lift of the Atlantic Ocean. This observation accompanies the story: "So it is by the life and lift of the Holy Spirit that our lives are energized, and that which is a hindrance is carried away, thus enabling our lives to be placed on a sure foundation."

When Jesus appeared to the disciples and said, "Receive the Holy Spirit," he was dramatically, by his very presence, confirming the incalculable power of God to be of such magnitude so as even to raise the dead! And if the power of God is of such inestimable magnitude, indeed the Holy Spirit is capable of lifting and removing burdens and weights of any nature as might come into our lives.

3. Consecration. It is not all greeting, invitation and confirmation. Something more was confirmed upon the awe-stricken, wonder-eyed band. Jesus said, "As the Father has sent me, even so I send you (v. 21)." The disciples were being consecrated into service imbued with the power of the Spirit, "Receive the Holy Spirit."

At age 30, Florence Nightingale made this entry into her diary: "I am now 30 years of age, the age at which Christ began his mission. Now, no more childish things, no more vain things. Now, Lord, let me think only of Thy will." Someone asked her years later, as her illustrious career and exceptional life began to wind down, "What is the secret of your good life?" She replied, "I can offer only one explanation and it is this, I have held nothing back from God." Jesus was asking the disciples to hold nothing back. The Holy Spirit stands ready now to consecrate us into his service, but we must hold nothing back.

There is a rather well-traveled poem which has been passed around to such extent that the author's name has become obscured. It is a somewhat unsettling bit of verse in that it relates an all-too-common response to the alternative of total consecration:

> "I'll go where you want me to go, dear Lord,
> real service is what I desire.
> I'll say what you want me to say, dear Lord,
> But don't ask me to sing in the choir.

I'll say what you want me to say, dear Lord,
I like to see things come to pass,
But don't ask me to teach girls and boys, dear Lord.
I'd rather just stay in my class.
I'll do what you want me to do, dear Lord,
I yearn for the kingdom to thrive.
I'll give you my nickels and dimes, dear Lord.
But please don't ask me to tithe.
I'll go where you want me to go, dear Lord.
I'll say what you want me to say.
I'm busy just now with myself, dear Lord,
I'll help you some other day.''

That which has not been dedicated cannot be consecrated. If something has not been given you, it is not really yours to use, much less bless into your service. The person whose mind is not made up is a candidate for compromise, but the consecrated life whose spirit has been dedicated to the leadership of the Holy Spirit can never be compromised.

United Methodist Bishop, Woodie White, was the preacher for the Little Rock annual conference. The last evening of the annual conference is always a highlight because of the ordination service. The sanctuary is always packed with people — lay delegates, clergy, families and friends who come to share in this high moment for the ordinands. Because the large attendance had created close seating throughout the sanctuary, and because I was one of the elders who would participate in the actual ordinations, I sat with the other participating elders at the front of the sanctuary, on the main floor, and to the side of the pulpit. Bishop White stood at the pulpit to preach. I could not see him. I could see his hands when he gestured. A large flower arrangement between the pulpit and chancel obscured my vision. I could hear his voice well enough and see his hands when they came into play, but I could not see the source. There was something mildly frustrating about that. It was like trying to watch television with someone standing in the way. The thought occurred to me of how frustrating it must be for thinking people who are looking for strong, convincing evidences of God. They can see the Bible, read it and hear it read. They can see the church and observe its program, see the gestures. But what people are really looking for is eye-to-eye contact with the Source. There are obstacles aplenty. Christian friends, the Bible says in so many ways that if the almighty God, and the manifestation of the Holy Spirit are ever to be visibly evident in human affairs, it will be through the human witness. The dedicated, consecrated witness! If religion is ever going to get beyond words and gestures, it will be because it has gotten into a person. You can be that person.

Jesus invited his disciples to receive the power of the Holy Spirit, to witness to the confirmation of his promises, and be consecrated into the service of the "Ever-Presence." As Christ spoke unto them, so I speak his words unto you: "Receive the Holy Spirit."

A Continuing Presence

Clarence Macartney tells of a certain Canadian river which flows through a forbidding chasm. Looming on either side of the river are rugged, uninviting crags which bear the names "Eternity" and "Trinity." Macartney suggests that the opposing crags invite an analogy (you understand of course, that to a preacher, most everything invites analogy). "Inseparable from any true conception of God," he says, "are always the two doctrines of God's eternity and God's trinity . . . The threefold experience of God the Father, God the Son, and God the Holy Spirit." The great preacher then goes on to conclude that both doctrines lie helplessly beyond human comprehension.

Let us narrow the orbit now to take up the matter of God's Trinity. We will allow Macartney's conclusion than an exhaustive theological comprehension of the Trinity may well be beyond our reach, but it is within our capacity to understand manifestations of God in all three persons. Norman MacLeod puts it simply: "There is a Father in heaven who loves us, a Brother-Saviour who died for us, and a Spirit who helps us." One would be hard pressed to improve upon such a practically stated formula. As a matter of fact, in so many ways throughout his life and ministry, Jesus advanced a strikingly similar interpretation and, as the time for his departure drew near, he addressed himself more and more to the work of the Spirit.

The gospel according to John contains a group of our Lord's sayings about the promised presence of the Holy Spirit (chapters 14-16). In 16:12-15, Jesus spoke with reserve and certainty. He did not tell the disciples everything. He could not. Not because he was unequipped for the occasion, but because they were: "I have yet many things to say to you, but you cannot bear them now (John 16:12)." No need to explain in future tense when they were experiencing difficulty in connecting present tense with past tense. Besides, Jesus had every confidence that the scattered pieces would eventually come together for them. Connections are always easier in retrospect. He could not tell them everything but he did tell them some things which, considering the words were later recalled and recorded, apparently impressed them.

I. The Certainty of the Spirit

The word "if" is a possibility word. It is fair comment to say that on the uphill side of life, the word most often refers to possibilities: "If I can just pass this examination, then I will qualify for a scholarship and if . . . ;" "If I invest $1,000 now in this certificate of deposit and if . . ." But on the downhill side of life, "if" is commonly used to sort back through what might have been: "If I had just gone to college and earned a degree . . . ;" "If I had moved when the company wanted me to move and if . . . ;" "If I had known then what I know now . . ." The word "if" always deals with possibilities in one form or another.

To point out the obvious, there is no "if" in our Lord's announcement concerning the activity of the Spirit. Not "if" the Spirit comes, but when the Spirit comes. No straining to see the flicker of a distant flame here. No reaching for hope-filled explanations. And, contrary to what some may suppose, Jesus was not announcing the "first time" appearance of a previously unheard of phenomena. Centuries before, the Spirit had "possessed" Gideon (Judges 6:34). The Spirit "came mightily upon Saul (1 Samuel 11:6)." Before that, the Spirit of God was obviously at work in the life of Joseph (Genesis 41:38). Before that, the Spirit "moved upon the face of the waters" at creation (Genesis 1:2). Isaiah had prophesied under the inspiration of the Spirit (Isaiah 61:1). The Spirit had come upon Jesus at his baptism (Matthew 3:16) and led him into the wilderness to be tempted by the devil (Matthew 4:1). Consequently, when Jesus addressed the disciples about the Spirit which "was to come," he was not preparing them for some new supernatural presence. He was impressing upon them that the continuing work of the Spirit would assume a more prominent role in God's redemptive activity. It was not a matter of "if," but a matter of "when." And the "when" was to be very soon!

In the days which followed, the disciples would witness the confirmation of everything Jesus had said many times over. In the centuries which have followed, the irrefutable evidence of the Spirit had confirmed the Lordship of Christ and baptized the commonlife of us all as a continuing presence.

The Spirit breathes upon our lives in many ways. Several years ago, a gentleman in his late 50s presented himself before a church conference board of ordained ministry as a candidate for the itinerant ministry. Members of the board were receptive to the applicant but, nonetheless, began pointing out the obvious considerations: his age, his limited education, the fact that his previous employment as a produce salesman and insurance agent would not substitute for a formal course of study which he would be required to undertake. Moreover, it was pointed out that his ministry would probably be confined to small, rural churches. He had already thought about all that. "Brethren, I just want to serve the Lord," he said, "and I believe the Lord can use me in those little churches."

I have never known a person of sweeter Christian countenance. His smile was totally disarming. Even his large frame seemed at times too small to contain such generous compassion. He possessed the rare gift of making everybody feel greater than they were. Time and again, he would make his way across a crowded floor of a conference or meeting just to grasp my hand, smile that beaming smile and say, "Hello, Doctor Powell." "I'm not a doctor of anything, Herb," I would tell him. "Well, you're a doctor to me," he insisted. It was always "Doctor Powell."

I loved that. I would go to meetings just hoping he would be there. He was a good man. A Christian man, exceedingly kind, and spoke only good of all whom he would meet. We wish that kind would live forever, but they don't. Herb suffered a heart attack and died five years later. Recently, I preached a sermon to the congregation I serve in Little Rock and referred to Herb in much the same way I have here. His marvelous spirit seemed appropriate for whatever it was I was attempting to illustrate. Following the service, I stood at the front door of the church greeting people as they made their way out. A man paused to comment, "I used to know a fellow just like the man you described and his name was Herb too. He was a produce salesman in Memphis who used to call on me." He thought back across the years for a moment, then asked, "Did you ever know a Herb _____?" I told him we were talking about the same person. Two days later, another church member came into my study and said, "As you were preaching Sunday, I remembered a man I knew named Herb who was just as you described, except he wasn't a preacher. He was our insurance agent. His name was Herb _____." I had not mentioned Herb's last name at any time during the sermon and yet, all three of us were speaking of the same person whose life had touched ours at different places. The two informants had confirmed a spirit which had been experienced personally. But more than that, they had confirmed the continuing presence of the Spirit which was apparent in the life of one who truly was "a friend of God."

Jesus promised the continuing presence of the Spirit. That promise is confirmed in our own experiences and relationships.

II. The Spirit as Guide

Jesus said the Spirit will "guide you into all the truth (John 16:13)." Truth is not always easily determined, particularly when it has been misrepresented. The government assures us that the tax dollars we provide are closely monitored and applied toward the cost of goods and services which are in our own best interest. However, disclosures about Pentagon spending and political scandal convey a tainted truth. Religious personalities preach about the things of God, condemn sin, appeal to our consciences, and invite us to surrender our lives to the leadership of the Spirit. It is a good formula, until it becomes corrupted by the one dispensing the formula. Then the "truth" as well as the vehicle of truth, becomes tangled. We are familiar with both tainted and tangled truth. So were the disciples. Here was Jesus saying one thing and the government, religious authorities, and circumstances saying another. Jesus had said, "I am the true vine," but the Pharisees and scribes said he was not of the vine of Israel. The government thought him to be a "bad seed" and circumstances indicated that the axe was soon to be laid to the root. Only a short time before, Jesus had said, "Now is the Son of Man glorified," but the Pharisees and scribes had insisted all along that the carpenter was attempting to glorify himself. Government officials claimed that he glorified no one, and circumstances were gathering more and more on the side of condemnation instead of glorification. Jesus had said, "Let not your hearts be troubled," but the disciples clearly discerned that his heart was troubled.

The light would eventually be turned up on it all. The tainted truth, the tangled truth, which required sorting out from the confusion would all come into focus for them: "I have yet many things to say to you, but you cannot bear them now. When the Spirit of truth comes, he will guide you into all truth."

The Spirit of truth reveals that which is of God. Witness the resurrection, Pentecost, the Scriptures, the church, goodness, beauty, truth, the providential involvement of the Spirit in our own lives, and all such confirmations as are in accordance with God's will. The Spirit of truth also reveals that which is not of God. Witness your daily newspaper. And when we observe that not even offenses within the church are exempt from God's scrutiny, we may be assured of the continuing work of the Spirit. Euripides once said, "When once I had seen the truth there was no drug that I could take to unsee it and lose again what I had seen." How much more revealing it must have been for the disciples following the Resurrection. Even more revealing for all who have personally experienced new life in the Spirit, reinforced by the testimonies of saints across the centuries.

The Spirit is not only a revealer of truth but a guiding presence, frequently best acknowledged by hindsight. Let me try to explain. William Cowper was an English poet and hymn-writer. He had studied law and was admitted to the bar in 1754. Strangely enough, he never practiced. Shy and gentle by nature, he was not emotionally equipped to deal with the stress and strain associated with the profession. He suffered intense fits of melancholy and spiritual despair. It is told that one evening he summoned a London cabby and directed him to drive to the Thames River. A heavy fog blanketed the city and for more than an hour, the cab driver cautiously drove along the obscured streets in search of the river. Little did the driver know that his noticeably impatient passenger had resolved to relieve his troubled mind by plunging into a watery grave. Cowper had weighed everything in the balances of life no longer seemed worth the bother. Angered by the delay and anxious to get on with his plan, Cowper lunged from the cab and set out to find the river on his own. He wandered and groped for what seemed like an eternity. Finally, he discovered himself standing at his own doorstep! Coincidence? Not in Cowper's judgment. He went directly to his room, took up pen and paper and wrote the words to the new familiar hymn: "God Moves in Mysterious Ways His Wonders to Perform." Again, the guiding presence of the Holy Spirit is frequently best acknowledged by hindsight. How many "coincidences" in life are eventually understood to be considerably beyond the level of "chance" in the long run? Oh, it has happened to you well enough. There were times when, perhaps for just a fleeting moment, you were overtaken in some circumstance by the urge to acknowledge "something." Something which had caused an impossible situation to take a turn for the better . . . just when your own finely laid calculations were at the point of collapse. Something happened. A new direction, a different perspective, another alternative emerged from the fog. Call it intuition. Call it inspired genius. Call it coincidence. Or, claim the promise our Lord made to his own, and call it the guidance of the Holy Spirit.

II. The Spirit Glorifies Christ

You are familiar with the towering signs commonly seen alongside interstate roadways boldly declaring the presence of a gasoline station. Such signs are impressive in themselves. We would think that it is no small feat just to erect, position, and secure the two enormously high metal posts, much less manipulate, balance, and afix a heavy sign at the very top. A gasoline station recently went out of business and removed its sky-sign. The two metal posts, however, were left intact. Somebody, I don't know who, has provided a new sign. It is a giant replica of an Arkansas automobile license plate with white background, red lettering. There are some changes. It is what amounts to a personalized tag. This one reads, "JESUS." The state slogan, "Land of Opportunity," has been changed to read, "Lord of Opportunity." Instead of a date of expiration, it reads, "Never Expires." We will not question the motive. The sign is clearly a serious, commendable gesture to glorify Christ, or "lift up his name." That is one way to do it. However, we will want to be sensitive to the countless other ways in which Christ is glorified at eye-level: (1) church-related hospitals, nursing homes, and institutions of higher learning glorify Christ daily. Additionally, whenever the hungry are fed, the hurting healed, and minds enlightened there is Christ glorified whether the vehicle is church-related; (2) a congregation gathers to sing praises, pray for pardon, and hear the Word of God proclaimed; (3) little children happily stand holding hands in a children's choir and sing, "I Am A Promise;" (4) a friend telephones or drops in on you unexpectedly to say,

51

"I heard you have been ill and I just wanted to check on you;" (5) you attend a Sunday school class or worship service and the teacher or minister puts together just the right combination of words that speaks in a personal way to a situation in your life.

Some of you are thinking now, "That list is so pitifully shallow. If you really want to hear how the Spirit touches lives, let me tell you about . . ." Yes! That is precisely what I want you to do. Recall that time, or times, in your life when you felt the breath of God mingling with your own breath; the mind of God inspiring your own mind; the Holy Spirit doing business with your spirit. Think now. Was it done for your sake or for the sake of the One who came that we might have life more abundantly? Was it done to lift your spirits or to lift up the name that is above every other name? Something inspires goodness, beauty, and truth. If that something is "coincidence," then it is a remarkably consistent coincidence, isn't it? The Scriptures, to my knowledge, do not contain the word, "coincidence." The reference used for centuries for continuing "coincidences" which bless, baptize, and enrich lives and glorify Christ, is the "Holy Spirit."

Jesus said, "When the Spirit of truth comes, he will glorify me, for he will take what is mine and declare it to you." Has the Spirit come into your life? In certainty, as your guide, enabling you to not only know the glorified Christ but to glorify Christ?

> "Into my heart, come into my heart, Lord Jesus.
> Come in today, come in to stay.
> Come into my heart, Lord Jesus."

Proper 4
Pentecost 2
Ordinary Time 9
Luke 7:1-10

Just Speak The Word

It is somewhere written down that many years ago a rider on horseback approached a group of soldiers attempting unsuccessfully to move a heavy piece of timber. A corporal was observed standing nearby, hands on hips, barking the order, "Heave. Heave." Despite repeated efforts, the soldiers were unable to accomplish the task. Apparently of the mind that the situation hinged upon his determined commands, the corporal persisted, "Heave. Heave." Addressing the corporal, the horseman asked, "Why don't you help them?" Straightening himself, the corporal snapped, "Because I am a corporal." The horseman dismounted, joined the soldiers and provided the extra muscle necessary to move the timber. He then climbed back upon his horse, looked the corporal in the eyes and said, "The next time your men need help, corporal, send for the commander-in-chief." The horseman was George Washington.

Give some people a little authority and they sometimes begin to think of themselves more highly than they ought to think. The transformation may not always be intentional. Authority, by its nature is capable of working a gradual change on one's personality. With this in mind, let us think now about the centurion referred to in our text.

Jesus entered Capernaum only to discover, as he would discover many times, that his reputation had preceded him. Oh, he had been in Capernaum before, well enough, but by now even those of rank and station had begun to take notice of him.

"Now a centurion had a slave who was dear to him, who was sick and at the point of death. When he heard of Jesus, he sent to him elders of the Jews, asking him to come and heal his slave (Luke 7:2, 3)."

53

A centurion commanded a Roman legion, numbering 100 men. It was not in a centurion's best interest to risk compromising his authority by making "requests." The privilege of "command" came with the position. The disposition to "demand" was expected. It is fair comment to say that the deportment of a Roman centurion could generally be characterized to resemble that of the corporal mentioned earlier, standing at a safe distance from a task, issuing orders that it be accomplished. The centurion mentioned in our text reminds Jesus of his importance: "For I am a man set under authority, with soldiers under me: and I say to one 'Go,' and he goes, and to another 'Come,' and he comes, and to my slave, 'Do this,' and he does it (7:8)." So, we may safely assume that when this man dispatched certain elders to ask Jesus to heal his slave, it was in the context of authority. Hardly. We will not want to rush past the fact that what we see happening here was a radical departure from our general characterization. This particular centurion jumps out at us because he is out of character. Jesus could not help but be impressed. He was further impressed when the Jewish elders volunteered, "He is worthy to have you do this for him, for he loves our nation, and he built us a synagogue (7:4, 5)." Jesus apparently was even more impressed when the centurion addressed him as "Lord," and confessed, "I am not worthy to have you come under my roof . . . but say the word, and let my servant be healed (7:6, 7)."

Little wonder that Jesus declared, "I have not witnessed such faith, even in all Israel." Moreover, as insensitive as it may sound, it would appear that the immediate healing of the servant is almost incidental to the faith-filled abandon exhibited by the centurion. He impresses us as a good man, compassionate, and humble. A man of authority, figuratively prostrating himself in the presence of Supreme authority.

Power of the Spoken Word

Jesus consented to the centurion's request. However, the centurion, fully aware of the power of the spoken word uttered by one in authority, responded by saying something to the effect, "Oh no, you don't need to trouble yourself more. I'm not worthy for you to come under my roof. Just speak the word and my servant will be healed." He is obviously convinced that if he has the power to command the lives of one hundred men with a word, beyond the shadow of a doubt, it is within the power of Jesus to dispel even the powers of darkness with but a word. "Speak the word only, and my servant will be healed."

Let us now draw the proposition that words have power closer to our own experience. A certain ministry of words has been given to each of us although we are not always faithful to speak them.

Words of reconciliation. Tempers flare and abrasive words are exchanged between you and a friend or loved one. Only moments before, the thought that such words would ever come from your mouth was inconceivable. Nerves are tense. Faces strain in hateful expressions. An awkward feeling presses down now upon the relationship. Words! Cutting and slashing words. See what they have done. And suspended there in your throat, dangling between passion and compassion, pride and reason, are two words waiting their time: "I'm sorry." Possibility words, sometimes impossible to say.

Words which remove fear. Here is a person sitting anxiously in a hospital waiting room. A friend or relative is undergoing a life-threatening operation. A multitude of "what ifs?" and "if onlys" race through a person's mind at a time like that. Finally, after what always seems like an inordinate length of time, the doctor enters the waiting room. "Everything went fine," he says, "No complications and the patient will be up in no time." What marvelous words! Just words, but see what they have done. They have removed the terrible weight of worry from tired shoulders, erased shadows which had crept in upon the soul, and replaced the unspoker fears with visible joy. Words have power!

When I was a little boy, it seemed everything on the street where I grew up was giant-sized. Especially trees. Tall,

55

spreading elm trees lined both sides of the street, overlapping to form a kind of leafy tunnel. The sidewalks too, stretched like a corridor in both directions.

One evening, following considerable debate, my parents reluctantly agreed that I would be allowed, for the first time, to attend the local theater without their accompaniment. The theater was only four blocks away, but that was not the point. The point was that finally, they were not going to chaperone me to and from the theater with all their grown-up guidance. It would be a small step for humankind, but a giant step for me. I was so ecstatic about this unexpected windfall of over-due freedom that it somehow escaped me that although the theater was only four blocks away, it was also four blocks back. The significance of that was the four blocks back would be in the dark.

I do not remember anything about the movie, but I do remember the walk home. The night was very dark. Thick, hovering trees obscured whatever welcome light there may have been from the lone streetlight. Shadows flickered and danced in every direction and grotesque, stoop-shouldered, long fin-gernailed ogres who prey upon little children lurked behind every tree. I could not see them but I knew they were there. I also knew that they would come upon me from behind, clutch me with their clammy hands and whisk me away to wherever those kinds of things whisk people away to. It is very difficult to tiptoe four blocks without breathing, looking in all direc-tions at the same time. Too frightened to walk, too afraid to run, my heart pounded against my shirt as if trying to break away and take its chances on its own. Now, there was only one block to go. Maybe I had a chance! But then I thought, "No they are going to wait until I am almost home and when I come to the front yard, maybe even the doorstep, they will capture me." Midway down the block, I saw it. The shadowy figure of a man in the middle of the sidewalk, coming slowly toward me. I knew there must be others closing in on me from their appointed places. Stopping in my tracks, I was just about to inform the neighborhood of my predicament when a voice said, "Something about to get you, boy?" It was my father's voice. Doxology and Hail Mary! He was coming up the street to meet me. My father's voice. Only words. But, my friends, I submit to you from personal experience, words can annihilate fear.

There is someone you know who needs to hear a word of assurance or encouragement. I do not know their names, but you know them and you know just such words they need to hear.

Words which remove loneliness. Leslie Weatherhead tells a rather pathetic story about Rupert Brooke, the English poet. Having boarded an ocean liner at Liverpool bound for New York, Brooke looked out on a sizable crowd of people lined along the quay to wave farewell to friends and family departing for America. Brooke had no friends in Liverpool and was suddenly overtaken by an almost unbearable sense of loneliness. Seeing a little street urchin standing alone on the quay, he rushed from the ship and made for the little boy. "What is your name?" he asked. "William," the surprised lad answered. "William, would you like to earn six-pence," Brooke asked. William was agreeable to do that. "All I want you to do," Brooke informed him, "is wave to me as the ship puts away." Weatherhead relates that Brooke never forgot the figure of the little urchin, waving a dirty handkerchief, delivering him from loneliness.

Sometimes that is about the sum of it, isn't it? We superficially wave a handkerchief to those we know to be lonely when we know what they would really appreciate is a sincere word. Loneliness is different from solitude. Solitude is intentional privacy. Loneliness is cricumstantial detachment. We could fine-tune the distinction, but we know the difference. More than that, we know the difference between detatchment and involvement. We know the difference between a playground filled with happy children and a nursing home filled with persons sorting through old photographs. We know the difference in home-bound shut-ins and the dedicated person or persons in your church committed to call on them. We know the difference in "waving a handkerchief" or giving a polite tip of the hat to one who is lonely instead of speaking words of fellowship and caring.

A hymn we sing from time to time contains the phrase, "Chords which were silent will vibrate once more." Taken in context of the total hymn, the phrase is understood easily enough, I suppose, but only recently have I come to fully appreciate extenuating implications pertaining to that particular combination of words. Dr. Charles L. Goodell produced a little volume not long after the turn of the century titled, *What Are You Worth?* In one of the chapters, he refers to a man standing beneath a great bell suspended high in a cathedral tower. The man patiently blew upon a flute, note by note, until at last a faint response from the bell was detected. He prolonged that specific note until the bell began to vibrate, every molecule awakened. The man then explains, "The deepest thing about that bell which no hand of mine could reach was the note to which it was tuned to respond." A musical note affecting an inanimate object, tuned to that particular note! Fascinating. I passed this information along to the music director of our church and asked her to explain it to me. "Oh, that is the overtone series," she smiled. She then proceeded to illustrate the principle on a piano by asking me to place my hand lightly upon certain keys. She would strike a particular key elsewhere on the keyboard and those beneath my hand vibrated in response. Keys were being activated because they had been tuned to the note effecting them. Does this suggest anything to us about the effect of caring words, spoken kindly to a lonely heart? It is a note to which the human heart is tuned to respond, and to speak such a word is to be in genuine ministry.

Words which heal. Ruth Graham, wife of evangelist Billy Graham, recalls how timely words healed a broken condition of her soul. Mrs. Graham's father served as a medical missionary to China. On one unforgettable day, bandits descended upon the city and presently became engaged in a shoot-out with the authorities. When the shooting was over, Mrs. Graham's

58

father worked for hours over one of the injured bandits, summoning all his medical skills in an effort to save the man's life. Finally, when it was apparent that the man would survive, the exhausted doctor carefully wrapped the patient's head wounds and took his leave. Mrs. Graham relates that three hours after her father had returned home, she passed beneath the city gate. Hanging from the gate was the head of the bandit her father had labored to save, bandages and all! Of that horrible moment, she says, "My faith was thrown into chaos. I didn't know what I believed anymore. In the years which followed, her spiritual dilemma progressively worsened. Later in life, while a student at Wheaton College, she had occasion to speak with one of her instructors and told him about her faith struggle. Dr. Gordon Clark was known to be a scholarly man, given to hard logic and unemotional brilliance. She fully expected him to respond to her with hard, cold facts. She had assumed correctly. However, she says that all she really remembers is the way he concealed his remarks, "Ruth, there is still the leap of faith." These words, removed from that particular conversation, perhaps do not light up the darkness for you or me, but they did for her. She then proceeded to take the blind leap of faith and, according to her own testimony, has known peace in her soul ever since. Dr. Clark had spoken the healing word!

Healing words — words which change circumstances, were very much a part of our Lord's ministry. We will not call them all up here, but we may be assured that the memory of the man healed of palsy never turned loose of the words, "Be of good cheer, your sins are forgiven." Nor did the woman healed of 12 torturous years of hemorrhaging ever forget the words, "Be of good comfort, your faith has made you whole." The sweetest words ever to be recalled by the adultress who was given a new lease on life, were: "Neither do I condemn you, go and sin no more." The thief on the cross drew his last breath on this side of eternity with the triumphant words ringing in his ears, "Truly, I say to you today, you shall be with me in Paradise." Words of healing, all.

To be sure, the healing ministry of Christ was unique but, as Christians, we have been given another grace; the witness of Christian fellowship with the ability to change another's condition, if only their attitude about their condition, by speaking a healing word. The writer of Proverbs said it best: "A word fitly spoken is like apples of gold in pictures of silver (25:11)."

Words of witness. A man came out of his house on his way to church one Sunday morning. Across the yard, his neighbor was loading his golf clubs into a station wagon. The neighbor said, "Henry, do you want to play golf with me today?" Henry, with an expression of self-righteous horror on his face, replied: "This is the Lord's day and I always go to church. Certainly I would not play golf with you today." After a moment of embarrassed silence, the golfer said: "You know Henry, I have often wondered about your church and I have always admired your devotion. You know also, this is the seventh time I have invited you to play golf with me, and you have never invited me to go to church with you."

Sometimes, the word of witness, like the other words we have mentioned, begs to be spoken.

"But say the word and let my servant be healed," the centurion appealed to Jesus. We admire his judgment, for the record shows that (1) his faith was not misplaced, and (2) his estimation of the power of the word was accurate. It was in such a spirit that you and I first came to Christ, was it not? Believing his word and convinced that in Christ there is life abundant. The presence of Christ in our own experiences continues to confirm that neither has our faith been misplaced nor the estimation of his power exaggerated. We know whom we have believed and are persuaded that he is able to keep that which we've committed unto him, not only against "that day," but today!

Look at that ancient soldier one last time. See him coming in behalf of another, engaging in ministry, putting together such a faith-filled, unrehearsed combination of words that our Lord could not help but take notice. Christ performed the greater ministry but the servant owes his healing to the centurion.

Let us be clear about it. We are not speaking of vocabulary or verbosity, but spiritual disposition. The disposition which embraces the strong spirit of Christ and dares to speak the word in behalf of another. There is someone to whom the sound of your voice is familiar, waiting to hear your voice now, speaking a word of reconciliation, fellowship, caring, healing, or witness.

> *"Let the words of my mouth and the meditation of my heart be acceptable in thy sight O Lord, my rock and my redeemer (Psalm 19:14)."*

So Close . . . But Yet So Far

Several summers ago, my wife and I had occasion to be in a little community in New York state which included the famous St. Elmo Hotel. Word had come to us that a former employee of the hotel, inspired by people and incidents encountered in and around the landmark building, had written a story titled, "St. Elmo's Fire." The story was eventually made into a movie by the same name. Naturally, we surveyed the premises for any sign of fire damage. Seeing none, we supposed that the fire at St. Elmo must have been confined to the interior. We wondered if a room had caught fire, a floor, a ceiling, a piece of furniture . . . what? Whatever it was apparently had been restored with masterful skill because there was no visible evidence of damage or repair. Oh well, at least we would be able to report to our friends that we had actually been in the building and close to the story.

A few weeks later, we saw the movie, *St. Elmo's Fire* in a local theater. We were confident that we would have the advantage of immediately recognizing certain things and be able to anticipate much of the story. We would soon discover, however, that although we had been in the hotel, we were painfully ignorant about the actual story being portrayed on the screen. As a matter of fact, the reason we had been unable to determine any fire damage is because there had been no fire in the first place.

Picture this one scene: a young lady, overwhelmed by life, on the verge of attempting suicide. A friend manages to get her attention long enough to explain that the trials and tribulations of life are not real. They are like "St. Elmo's Fire," only appearing to be real.

Following the movie, I went immediately to the encyclopedia and read: "St. Elmo's fire is the name given to a round

flash of light that is seen around ships in a thunderstorm."
The flash of light is so named because it gives the appearance
of fire. In stormy weather, this charge of electricity may be
seen around airplanes, masts of ships, steeple tops, and tree
tops . . . as well as around horses' manes and people's heads!
St. Erasmus (St. Elmo, for short) was the patron saint of
Mediterranean sailors.

We had missed the pcint completely. Familiar with
peripheral associations, yes; but there was more, much more.

Although we may be "close to the story," it is usually a
good idea to allow for further light.

I. Premature Conclusions

The great multitude had been with Jesus and the 12 for
better part of the day. Jesus had spoken to them about the
kingdom of God and healed those who had need of healing.
Now, the sun was low in the sky and it was time to think of
physical provisions. The disciples are to be commended for
approaching Jesus on behalf of the faithful who had stayed
for the duration, rather than referring to their own fatigue and
hunger, "And the 12 came and said to him, 'Send the crowd
away, to go into the villages and country round about, to lodge
and get provision, for we are here in a lonely place.' " They
were considerate. We will give them that. But as the conversation progressed, there was some indication that they had not
taken everything into account. Jesus acknowledged their concern with an unexpected reply, "You give them something to
eat." Perhaps Jesus had been so involved with teaching and
healing that he had not had the opportunity to accurately as-
sess the situation. They would inform him, "We have no more
than five loaves and two fish, unless we are to go and buy food
for all these people (for the men alone numbered about
5,000)." It was a logical conclusion, wasn't it? Logical, yes,
but premature.

64

"And he said to his disciples, 'Make them sit down in companies, about 50 each.' And they did so, and made them all sit down. And taking the five loaves and the two fish he looked up to heaven, and blessed and broke them, and gave them to the disciples to set before the crowd. And all ate and were satisfied. And they took up what was left over, 12 baskets of broken pieces (9:14b-17)."

Illogical arithmetic: 5 (loaves) times 2 (fish) equal in excess of 5,000 (servings), with a remainder of 12 (baskets). We will not dwell on the numbers however, for they are incidental to the primary revelation. The disciples were in the company of one who had direct access to the incalculable abundance of God! They should have anticipated that the situation would be handled. They were familiar with his manner, accustomed to his revolutionary teachings about the kingdom, and eyewitnesses to numerous previous miracles. They were "close to the story," but had missed it. They had prematurely concluded that there was not the wherewithal to meet the need. Even for them, the lesson "Everything is possible for him who believes" would be hard for the learning.

Our assessments are often lacking. There is a much-traveled story about a poor derelict whom police discovered crumpled on the streets of Paris many years ago. The man was in a bad way. Supposing him to be ill, or inebriated to the point of danger — they did not know — they immediately transported him to the nearest hospital. In a matter of moments, he was placed upon a table in the emergency room and surrounded by doctors. The doctors, speaking in Latin, conferred with one another. Finally, one of them said, "What shall we do with this worthless wretch?" Much to their surprise, the man on the table weakly replied in flawless Latin: "Gentlemen, do not call him worthless for whom Christ has died." He, too, had been a doctor and, as they so rudely discovered, there was more to his story than they had judged. Such is usually the case, isn't it? I remember reading somewhere that it is difficult to determine whether a ship's deck is in disarray due to neglect or because of a storm.

We have received the sacrament of holy communion many times. We know that it originated in the upper room on the night that Jesus was betrayed. We are familiar with the symbolic nature of the elements, and understand the significance of the words spoken in the ritual. Because we have received the sacrament and know something about historical and theological meanings, we feel "close to the story." That is good. However, our text suggests that there may be additional components to the sacrament which we have not always taken into account.

S. MacLean Gilmour suggests that the incident of the multiplication of the loaves and fish is a miracle story which has come to be regarded as a prototype of the eucharist. In the same volume, John Knox remarks that the ritual actions which accompanied the distribution of the food confirms a relationship to the meal in the upper room, "Here is an anticipation of the last supper and a symbol of the reality of the church and Christ as the Lord of life." It comes as no surprise that scattered bits and pieces of information and random incidents are eventually understood to be snuggly fit together in the Bible's story. This piece must not be omitted:

> *"A man came from Baalshalishah, bringing the man of God bread of the first fruits, twenty loaves of barley, and fresh ears of grain in his sack. And Elisha said, 'Give to the men that they may eat.' But his servant said, 'How am I to set this before a hundred men?' So he repeated, 'Give them to the men, that they may eat, for thus says the Lord. "They shall eat and have some left." ' So he set it before them. And they ate, and had some left according to the word of the Lord (2 Kings 4:42-44)."*

To be sure, Jesus fed more than Elisha, but Jesus was "greater than Elisha." That was the point! Greater than Elisha or Elijah, or any of the prophets. But unmistakably connected to the prophets and the intentional, consistent redemptive activity of God. Second Kings 4:42-44 is not just an isolated Old Testament miracle story. The feeding of the 5,000 is not just an isolated New Testament miracle story. The supper in the upper room is not independent unto itself. The first two incidents provide a foretaste of the third.

The disciples prematurely concluded that Jesus could not possibly feed the 5,000 hungry people with five loaves and two fish. They were so very close to the story but so far from following the main plot. We know the feeling.

II. Underestimating Resources

When all available resources were collected and brought to Jesus, the supply did not meet the demand, at least not until the supply had been blessed. The blessing did it! Like the disciples, we do not always take the possibilities of the blessing into account, nor are we always accurate in our estimates of resources. Perhaps you have heard the story of the football coach who had two quarterbacks. The first team quarterback was gifted, aggressive, and a born leader. The second string quarterback was, let us say, limited. Oh, he was athletic enough but unfortunately, his ignorance was only surpassed by his stupidity. The championship game was in progress, the score was tied, the home team had the ball, and the clock was ticking down. An opposing player broke through the line of scrimmage and slammed the star quarterback to the ground with such force that the signal-caller had to leave the game. Time was running out. The coach had no choice but to put in the back-up. The substitute trotted onto the field, huddled the team, and strode up to the line of scrimmage. Surveying the opposing team, and much to everyone's surprise, he changed the play at the line. The ball was snapped, the quarterback handed it off to the half-back who busted up the middle and sped all the way into the end zone with the winning touchdown! An amazing play. Moments later, in the ecstatic dressing room, the coach grabbed his second-team quarterback by the shoulder pads and said, "Son, that was great! How did you know to call that play?" The boy said, "Uh, well coach, it weren't easy. I got up to the line and looked across at two of the biggest players I've ever seen and I seen their numbers. One of 'em was wearing a six and the other one was wearing a seven, so I just added them numbers together and got fourteen and called number fourteen." The coach hesitated a moment and said, "But son, six and seven make 13." The boy, quite unmoved by the correction, said, "You know what coach? If I was as smart as you, we would have lost the game." Things do not always add up the way they are supposed to, do they?

See in your mind's eye a young lad, armed only with a slingshot and five smooth river stones going out to do battle with Goliath, the Philistine giant. King Saul had tried to dissuade David by saying, "You are not able to go against the Philistine to fight with him. You are but a youth and he is a man of war from his youth (1 Samuel 17:33)." It just didn't add up. But when the dust had settled over the scene,

> "So David prevailed over the Philistine with a sling and with a stone, and struck the Philistine, and killed him; there was no sword in the hand of David (1 Samuel 17:50)."

Saul had underestimated the available resources. A dynamic was at work that he had not taken into account.

Do you know the name, Charles A. Tindley? Charles was the son of a slave and became an orphan while still a young boy. He was passed around from farm to farm, working for one landowner, then another. Some were kind but, more often than not, the lad was dealt with harshly. Charles, like other farm laborers, was not allowed to own a book or learn how to read and write. One day on his way to the field, he noticed a small piece of newspaper lying by the side of the road. Inconspicuously, he picked it up and stuffed it inside his shirt. In time, he would collect many such bits and pieces. At night, when all the others were asleep, he would burn a pinecone and, hovering over it to hide the light, struggle to understand the words. In this manner, Charles eventually taught himself to read. At some point in his youth, he came into possession of a Bible, which his inquisitive mind eagerly consumed. The day would come when he determined to go to church regardless of the consequences. A work shirt was washed in a ditch and draped over a limb to dry. One Sunday morning, he put on the shirt, dusted off his pants, washed his feet in a puddle of water, and made for the church. When he arrived, he slipped in the door, took a deep breath, and gripped his Bible with both hands. The minister asked all the little children to come forward to the front pew and read from their Bibles. Charles went forward. Several people hissed and one person actually reached out in an attempt to grab him. He would not be denied. The children inched along laboriously with their Bible readings until they had all read their favorite passages. It was Charles' time. Without stammering or hesitation, he read verse after verse and would have completed an entire chapter had he not been interrupted by the minister "in the interest of time."

Charles A. Tindley was admitted to the Methodist ministry in 1885. He served the same church for several years where he had previously worked as a janitor. He was an illustrious member of the Philadelphia Conference. He wrote numerous hymns and doubtless had his early life in mind when he wrote, "Stand By Me." Only he knows how many times he must have recited to himself the lines, "When my faith is tossed about like a ship upon the sea, thou who rulest winds and waters, stand by me."

It would have been easy to look at the young orphan boy and categorically underestimate the potential. But God appraised the available resources, blessed them, and shaped them into a doctor of divinity, hymn writer, loving pastor, and powerful preacher who led many to Christ.

The disciples saw only five hard loaves and two fish, long out of the water. Saul had seen only a shepherd boy with a hand-full of stones and a home-made slingshot. And many were they who looked at a little barefoot orphan boy and saw only a field hand. None of the estimations were accurate because everything had not been taken into account. God's blessing of the resources, using what was available — such as it was — made the difference. It always does.

III. Mistaken Impressions

Don't you see, just being close to a situation doesn't necessarily mean we have gathered it all in! Recently, my wife and I were driving down one of the highways leading into Little Rock. As we approached the city limits, we were passed from behind by a white van with writing on the windows. Written in large letters on the passenger side was the word, "Poison." An arrow pointing straight ahead underlined the word. As the van moved in front of us, we could see another word on the rear window, "Tesla." At first, I thought it was "Tulsa," . . . you know, one of those "Tulsa or Bust" signs, but the spelling was all wrong and Tulsa was in the opposite direction. "Tesla . . . Poison?" In a moment, I asked my wife, "Does any of that make any sense to you?" The words did not compute with her either. I reasoned to myself that one word was probably an acrostic or code name for something and the other was possibly the work of a dedicated environmentalist trying to make a statement about the atmosphere. The following morning, I read in the *Arkansas Gazette* that two heavy-metal rock groups, Tesla and Poison, had played to 10,000 fans in Barton Coliseum the night before. Now, we live in Little Rock, listen to the radio, read the newspaper, and our parsonage is located relatively close to Barton Coliseum. We were, let us say, close to a situation, the meaning of which simply out-distanced us.

It has happened before — this business of "mistaken impressions." It has happened to you, hasn't it? We are in good company. The disciples were of the mind that the multitude would not be fed. Saul, impressed with little David's bravery but sad for the odds, judged in Goliath's favor. Elisha's servant asked, "How am I to set 20 loaves of barley and a sack of grain before a hundred hungry men?" Premature conclusions, inaccurate estimations, mistaken impressions — they jump out at us like sparks from a well-kindled fire.

Christian friends, allow for the possibility that, although we have received the sacrament of holy communion many times, there is still more. More to ponder, more to experience.

We partake of the sacrament:

(1) in response to Christ's command. ". . . And when he had given thanks, he broke it (bread), and said, 'This is my body which is for you. Do this in remembrance of me.' In the same way also the cup, after supper, saying, 'This cup is the new covenant in my blood. Do this, as often as you drink it, in remembrance of me' (1 Corinthians 11:24, 25).''

(2) in the knowledge that God blesses our lives and can transform circumstances. Paul said, "Do not be conformed to this world but be transformed by the renewal of your mind, that you may prove what is the will of God, what is good and acceptable and perfect (Romans 12:2).''

(3) remembering that God is able to use what is available and use it abundantly. Jesus said, "I have come that you may have life and have it more abundantly (John 10:10).''

(4) to experience Christ's presence, Jesus said, "Where two or three are gathered together in my name, there am I in the midst of them (Matthew 18:20).''

(5) to receive spiritual food for our journeys and cleansing for our souls. Paul said, "Since we have these promises, beloved, let us cleanse ourselves from every defilement of body and spirit, and make holiness perfect in the fear of God (2 Corinthians 7:1).''

May we not only be "close" now to this sacrament, but genuinely experience it.

But God Can

She was all alone now, this widow of Nain. The Scriptures make no mention that she had brothers or sisters or other family members. They surely would have been with her, consoling her, moving slowly along in the sad procession. A "large crowd from the city was with her." We are grateful for that. Sometime before, we don't know how long, she had stood by the grave of her husband and now the lifeless body of her only son was being carried out of the city. Only a widowed parent can know the grief that poor woman was feeling. As with any of the deep things of life, we cannot put her feelings into words, but we can appreciate her unutterable grief. The plain, indelicate truth is that no parent wants to live long enough to bury a son or daughter. We want to be mercifully spared that . . . at least that.

> "As he (Jesus) drew near to the gate of the city, behold, a man who had died was being carried out, the only son of his mother, and she was a widow (v. 12)."

So, you see, the circumstances for something wonderful happening could not have been more forbidding. And that is what makes what did happen all the more wonderful.

> "And when the Lord saw her, he had compassion on her and said to her, 'Do not weep.' And he came and touched the bier, and the bearers stood still. And he said, 'Young man, I say to you, arise.' And the dead man sat up and began to speak. And he gave him to his mother (vv. 13-15)."

73

The raising of the dead. We encounter it three times in our Lord's ministry. In addition to the widow's son, there was the daughter of Jairus (Matthew 9:18f) and Lazarus (John 11).

The orbit widens. Our understanding of God's actuality and potentiality expands.

It was Friedrich Nietzsche who said, "Man is a recurring decimal. You can never work him out on paper. You may divide and divide until your heart is content, but each figure you get, so far from beginning to end, is simply a new beginning." I suppose the antithesis of this continuing decimal theory would be to say, "Man is a period, or an exclamation point. This and nothing more."

It will be much more to your relief that I do not wish to pursue this. I just find the symbols of decimals, periods, and exclamation points interesting because I have often thought that a fitting symbol for God would be the ampersand — that peculiar little symbol (&) commonly used in place of the word "and" — for whatever is proclaimed about God must always end with the word "and." God is always more than we can know or express.

Millions of books about God are in circulation throughout the world. If all of these books were to be placed together in one great heap, it would surely seem that everything which could be written about God has been expressed in every conceivable combinations of words. However, the last page of every book could appropriately be inscribed with the word "and" for God is always more than we set to the page.

Millions of testimonies about God touching human lives have been presented. And just when you may think you have heard them all, someone says, "And listen to this."

Countless systematic theologies have meticulously been formulated, as well as learned, sophisticated perspectives about God and God's Word. Even so, there will always be another observation, another word aching to be said.

Just when it appears that God has blessed our lives in every conceivable way, he comes in a new way. There is always more.

Any definition of God must end with an ampersand, allowing for the "furthermore," for God was, and is, and shall be.

This thought was in the mind of the apostle Paul when he wrote: "Who shall separate us from the love of Christ? Shall tribulation, or distress, or persecution, or famine, or nakedness, or peril, or sword? . . . No, in all these things we are more than conquerors through him who loved us. For I am sure that neither death, nor life, nor angels, nor principalities, nor things present, nor things to come . . . nor anything else in all creation will be able to separate us from the love of God in Christ Jesus our Lord (Romans 8:35-39)." It is fair comment to paraphrase Paul's words to say, "I cannot overcome tribulation, distress, persecution, things present or things to come in my life, but God can." I challenge you now to think of any three words in the human language more wonderfully exciting than these: but God can! I challenge you to think of any one person in human history to whom this was more dramatically revealed than the widow of Nain. In her son's funeral procession one moment, praising God for his resurrection the next. It was unnecessary for Jesus to say to her, as he would later say to a certain rich man, "What is impossible with man is possible with God (John 18:27)." She knew.

But God can! What a marvelous thing to know and believe, especially since our present generation places such a premium on self-help and self-assertion. The emphasis is upon what "we" can do. We are told that we can determine our own security with stocks, bonds, certificates of deposit, and wise investments. We are told that we can guarantee our health by going to a health spa, swimming, jogging, playing tennis, or dieting. We are told that we can favorably impact our personal appearance by going to a tanning booth, having cosmetic make-overs, or plastic surgery. We can tuck this in, relocate that, remove something else altogether, and spray on all kinds of fragrances to create an impression and reinforce confidence. We are told that we can live good, look good, and even go to a self-help group and "be" good.

All things are wonderful. But we know in private, when we take counsel with ourselves, that there is also that which we cannot do: (1) we cannot control our lives. Just when we think it is under control, something comes along and takes the control away from us, (2) we cannot do God's will alone. We know, because we have tried, (3) we cannot release the power of the Holy Spirit upon our lives. We have difficulty keeping our own spirits high. We cannot do any of these things which count for now and all eternity, but God can!

It is when we conceive God as a "period" or "exclamation point" (convinced that God is this and no more) instead of "ampersand" that we lose our sense of anxious expectation and believing faith. Genesis 17 records that Abraham was informed in his old age that he was going to be a father. He laughed so hard that he literally fell down on his face, saying, "Shall a son be born to him that is 100 years old, and shall Sarah bear a child at 90?" A similar story is found in the first chapter of Luke. Zechariah and Elizabeth, old in years, received the unbelievable news that they were to become parents of a son. Zechariah felt moved to bring the matter into focus, "But I am an old man and my wife is stricken in years."

Abraham and Zechariah were not what we would call "possibility thinkers" in their old age. They were tired and the light was gone out of their eyes. At their age, they were more conscious of limitations, conclusions, and "periods" than they were possibilities. "It cannot happen," they responded. But God said, "It is within my will and it not only can, it shall," and it did. Do not minimize this thought: but God can.

We are always the wrong age to do something for the kingdom, aren't we? It seems we are either too young or too old. God called Jeremiah to be a prophet to the nations. Immediately, Jeremiah disqualified himself account of his age, "Oh Lord God, I cannot speak, for I am only a youth." What a pity. God was not simply calling him to address a tribe or a community, or even a district, but raising him up to be a witness to the "nations." How could God commit such an obvious mistake as to place so staggering a responsibility upon a youth? We can almost hear Jeremiah thinking, "I cannot command listeners, I cannot pronounce prophetic words, and I cannot conceive how you could possibly use me." And then it is as if God addressed Jeremiah's reluctance by replying, "I know you can't, but I can!"

> *"Do not say, 'I am only a youth'; for to all to whom I send you you shall go, and whatever I command you you shall speak. Be not afraid of them, for I am with you to deliver you (Jeremiah 1:7, 8)."*

If it is not age, it is something else. Moses declined God's call, citing his lack of eloquence (Exodus 4:10). Knowing perhaps that eloquence is not a prerequisite to witness, he added weight to the matter by saying, "I am slow of speech and slow of tongue." The bottom line to Moses' excuse is, "I cannot speak." God's reply: "I know you can't, but I can,"

> *"Who has made man's mouth? Who makes him dumb, or deaf, or seeing, or blind? Is it not I, the Lord? Now, therefore go, and I will be with your mouth and teach you what you shall speak (Exodus 4:11, 12)."*

Isaiah attempted to beg out of his calling by calling God's attention to the fact that he was a sinner. We expect that Isaiah felt that he had neutralized the call to prophecy with that confession. Jeremiah's age had not really been an issue. Moses' concern about his speech was of little concern to God. But there was no getting around the fact that Isaiah was correct. He was a sinner. Moreover, he could use his sinful condition to his advantage by using it for leverage. "Why, God, I can't be a prophet because I am a sinner." Read Isaiah 6:5 and see him become ever so humble in the presence of holiness. But then, read on and see how he was led beyond conviction to submission. It was as if God had declared, "Yes, you are a sinner and you do dwell in the midst of sinners. You cannot do anything about the fact of your sin nor their sin, but I can!"

At the risk of appearing to insult our intelligence, let us be clear about what dramatic thing we are proposing here. We are advancing Christ's proclamation, "What is impossible with man is possible with God (John 18;27)" and understanding them to mean, but God can! The widow of Nain would wonder why it is so difficult for us to absorb this obvious truth, as would Jeremiah, Moses, and a host of others across the centuries.

Sparks now leap from the fire:

(1) God can if we believe God can. The Book of Judges records a marvelous story of unreserved faith in the providence of God. Gideon and his army were camped beside the spring of Harod, just to the south of the Midianite encampment. At the appointed time, 32,000 Israelites would descend upon the enemy's superior forces and pray that their efforts would prevail. It is not a good feeling going against an adversary knowing the odds are against you. On the other hand, to triumph against the odds creates heroes.

God was not in search of heroes. "The Lord spoke to Gideon and said, 'The people with you are too many for me to give the Midianites into their land, lest Israel vaunt themselves against me' (Judges 7:2)." Brute strength and military prowess would only serve to obscure God's hand in the matter. Gideon was instructed to allow those who were fearful and trembling to go home. Apparently, some were there against their better judgment anyway because 22,000 went home. This reduced the Israelite army to 10,000. The odds were not pitifully overwhelming. However, God spoke again to Gideon and insisted that the soldiers still numbered too many! Just a minute. This is not only a time for an inventory of strength but also of one's belief in what God is able to accomplish. Gideon did not hesitate. "Take the men down to the water," God said, "and separate those who lap the water like dogs from those who kneel down to drink." And the number of those who lapped was 300. God then declared, "With the 300 I will deliver you." The significance of this number comes into clearer focus when we take into account how the Scriptures describe the Midianite army: "(they) lay along the valley like locusts for multitude; and their camels were without number, as the sand which is upon the seashore for a multitude; and their camels were without number, as the sand which is upon the seashore for a multitude (7:12)."

Gideon divided the 300 into three companies of 100. It does not require a military genius to determine that this would leave one side unprotected, even if the modest handfuls could cover the other three.

This was the battle plan: the 300 would carry no weapons in their hands and engage in no hand-to-hand conflict with the Midianites. Each soldier carried a trumpet in his right hand and a jar containing a lighted torch in his left. Allow the absurdity of the situation to settle into your consciousness. A diminished, token force, armed only with trumpets and earthen jars containing torches. Isn't it possible that at least one soldier may have felt inclined to remind Gideon that Israel was preparing for war instead of a midnight parade?

At Gideon's command, the 300 surrounded the Midianite camp. At the signal, the trumpets were blown, the jars loudly smashed, and each man cried out at the top of his voice, "A sword for the Lord and for Gideon!" To suggest that Gideon had utilized the element of surprise would be to understate the matter. The Midianites were so astonished and confused that they took up their swords against each other and fled in absolute bewilderment. The battle had gone to the hosts of the Lord. Let us take notice of that fact. Three hundred unarmed soldiers cannot route thousands who are armed. But God can! People cannot prevail against an impossible situation, regardless of the nature of the situation, but God can! Gideon and the 300 believed God could, and he did. God can if we believe God can!"

There are times when our own resources are diminished. Our strength is spent. All of the marvelous things which we know count for nothing. We are out of ideas. We are involuntarily disarmed, physically and mentally immobilized. Like the Israelites in the valley of Moreh, the odds are against us and we are vulnerable on every side. There is no way we can overcome a hopeless situation. But God can.

I do not know exactly what particular incident or theological concept the writer of the old hymn, "Only Believe," had in mind but Gideon and the 3000 most certainly could inspire such words: "Only believe, only believe. All things are possible, only believe." God can if we believe God can.

(2) God can if we will let him. It is not so much a matter of giving God permission as it is getting out of God's way. We want to be in front, call the plays, take charge, and manage our own affairs. That is not surprising, especially since our generation has been raised on the attitude of "You can if you believe you can." It is a good thought except it is limited on every side by our humanity.

Catherine Marshall tells in one of her books about how devastated she was when, following a routine physical examination, she was informed that she had tuberculosis. She was not mentally prepared for that. No one ever is. She was ordered to bed 24 hours a day indefinitely. Fifteen months later, she had gained 15 pounds. After a year and a half in bed, there was no noticeable progress. It was at this point that tormenting thoughts began innundating her mind. Had she committed some unforgivable sin at sometime in her life? Had she wronged someone and needed to make things right with them? Was there something about her life so offensive to God that her prayers were being short-circuited? What could she do? She apologized to her husband for everything she could think to apologize for. She wrote acquaintances and purged her conscience. She prayed to God and asked what else she could do. What else could she do? Finally, one day she conceded defeat. She had run out of ideas. She had fought and struggled, and worried until there was nothing left. Standing by her bedroom window, she prayed. The prayer, recorded in her diary, was: "From this moment I promise that I'll try to do whatever you tell me for the rest of my life, insofar as you'll make it clear to me what your wishes are. I'm weak and many times I'll probably renege on this. But Lord, you'll have to help me with that too." That was the moment of surrender. She got out of the way. Within six weeks, her condition improved until she was taking walks, working in the garden, making jelly, and eventually resumed her "normal life."

Catherine Marshall's story may be summarized in these words: God can, if we will let him.

(3) God can, but it may require our help as well as our consent. This past summer my wife and I had occasion to be in Tuscumbia, Alabama. Having passed through the city numerous times en route to somewhere else, we decided that this would be the time we would finally take the time to visit the home of Helen Keller. Oddly enough, the two of us were the only visitors on the premises at that particular time, so the tour guide was able to accommodate our slow pace as well as our numerous questions. "Here," she said, "is the living room and Helen's little chair." I was not particularly interested in the little chair, nor the kitchen, nor the bedrooms, nor any of the several awards in the trophy room. I was only mildly interested in the little cottage at the side of the house where Helen and her teacher lived during the time of her intense instruction. What I wanted to see was the pump. Finally, there it was just outside the back door of the main house. The place where the miracle happened. You know the story of how it was there that Helen first related the feel of water with the word "water" spoken by her teacher. Oh, she could not hear the word, but she could "feel" the word being spoken by placing her hand on her teacher's mouth and throat. I stood by the pump for a while and thought to myself, "Thank God for Anne Sullivan." Anne Sullivan (herself, partially blind) assumed the "impossible" task of teaching a blind deaf-mute child. We can only imagine how many times she must have thought, I cannot do this" as she encountered one frustration after another. But God could, and she would be God's agent. God was at the pump. God was in the inspiration of the moment, and Anne Sullivan had served as God's partner in the moment of miracle.

God can, if we believe God can, if we will let him, and be available to help if necessary.

We have come a long way from the window of Nain. But the joyous discovery which she experienced in her soul is the thing we have carried with us through all of us. We have stated it over and over in numerous ways. We have focalized our thoughts to this one: but God can!

And whether this sermon concludes with a "period" or an "ampersand" depends now upon you. Whether we have "focalized" a thought or "internalized" a thought depends upon you.

Perhaps, even now, you are thinking of some situation in your life which you wish you had control over, but you cannot get hold of it. Here is some decision which you cannot resolve. There is something you want to change for the better but you cannot. You are under the spiritual conviction that God has a plan for your life but you cannot bring it into focus?

You say to yourself, I have this need but I can continue on from here without resolving it and no one can tell the difference. But God can!

You say, "Preacher, you can't do anything about any of this. That is correct. I cannot. But God can. And the good news is that God will, if we believe him, and will let him!

Tears And Ointment

Senator William Proximire (D-Wisconsin) regularly delights the general public by awarding his now-famous "Golden Fleece Award" to some government committee or agency which, because of some redundant high-dollar project, has achieved recognition for excelling in flagrant, wasteful, unnecessary spending. Senator Proximire gets our attention because he illuminates a subject of interest to us all: how money is spent. We do not like to spend more than we have to and have little tolerance for irresponsible, reckless spending wherever it occurs. "Throwing money out in the yard" and "pouring sand down a rat hole" are expressions which we hope to successfully avoid having applied to ourselves. It really doesn't matter whether we speak of it as stewardship, frugality, or practicality. Wasteful spending is offensive to anyone who attempts to be responsible with personal resources.

Extravagance

Extravagance, or even what appears to be extravagance, does not go down well. We need to remember that whether we read of the woman anointing Jesus' head (Matthew 26:6f) or the woman anointing his feet (Luke 7:36f). It has been suggested that the two accounts refer to the same incident. I do not know. However, I do know this:

• The anointing recorded by Matthew occurred at Bethany. In Luke it was the city of Nain.
• In Matthew, the host is Simon the Leper. In Luke, Simon the Pharisee.

- Matthew refers to "a woman." Luke calls her "a woman of the streets."
- In Matthew, the woman pours the ointment over Jesus' head. In Luke, the ointment is applied to his feet.
- In Matthew, the disciples whine about wasted perfume. In Luke, the Pharisee mutters under his breath about Jesus wasting his time and emotion on an 'undeserving' woman.

Both accounts contain complaints about that thing which is near and dear to each of us: wasted resources! Consequently, let us not be too nasty in our condemnation of the disciples and the Pharisee. They were only making justifiable observations. They did have a point. We will allow that.

We will part company now with Matthew's account and take up the woman in Luke who washed Jesus' feet with her tears, dried them with her hair, and anointed them with ointment. How could she be so bold as to intrude into the residence of a monitor of righteousness? The contrast between her and others in the room would be immediately disconcerting. Why such an extravagant outpouring at that particular time? (How would you feel if you were entertaining a guest in your home and someone barged in uninvited and unannounced, not to see you, but your guest, and proceeded to rearrange the agenda? Why did she feel so constrained to be attentive to Jesus when the righteous Pharisee had neglected to be totally courteous?

The Intrusion

It was an intrusion, no doubt about that. Rudeness, however, is not nearly so prominent here as is determination, perhaps even desperation. When one's mind is locked-in on a single thought and the will is riveted to the pursuit of that thought, social niceties and topical etiquette are not always observed. Just because the woman was of ill repute is no sign that she did not know how to be civil. Apparently, she had only one thing on her mind: getting to Jesus. Why? It is rather commonly held among commentators that the fact the woman came "prepared" to anoint Jesus indicates that the incident was not just a spontaneous burst of emotion. In all likelihood, she had heard Jesus preach, witnessed a miracle, or had her life touched in some manner by him to the point of experiencing forgiveness of her sins. Full of joyful gratitude, and determined to do something for the one who had done so much for her, she made straightway for Jesus.

There is an old story about the Greek Marathon. Muscular, conditioned runners paced nervously near the starting line for the long-distance race. The time was near. They "shook out" their muscles, inhaled deeply, and put on their "game faces." In the midst of it all, a young stranger took his place at the starting line. His physique was awesome. Taking no notice of the other contestants, he stared straight ahead. Two prizes would be awarded the winner of the Marathon: a magnificent bouquet of flowers and the honor of standing beside the king until the conclusion of other contests. There seemed to be no question among the runners about who would win the prize. It is alleged that the stranger was offered money not to run. Someone else attempted to bribe him with property. Refusing the offers, he toed the mark and awaited the signal to run. When the signal was given, he was the first away. At the finish line, he was the first to cross, well ahead of the rest. When it was all done, someone asked the young man if he thought the flowers were worth as much as the money and property he had refused. He replied, "I did not enter the race for the flowers. I ran so that I could stand beside my king!"

Again, the woman who "intruded" into the Pharisee's house apparently had one thing on her mind. She wanted to stand beside her king.

The Timing

Could not the woman have chosen a more appropriate opportunity to express the overflow of her soul? Perhaps. But the fact of the matter is, she did not know that she would have any other opportunity, appropriate or not. Jesus' whereabouts were unpredictable. He was here one moment, gone the next. In a village one day, preaching from a fishing boat the next. Sometimes he moved openly among the people, at other times he moved in the shadows. How was she to know when or where she would catch up to him again? So, she took advantage of the opportunity when it presented itself at the home of Simon the Pharisee. Not an ideal, private, calculated opportunity, but an opportunity. Catch as catch can.

The Right Time

Wallace D. Chappell tells that following one of his sermons a little girl came to the front of the church to meet him. He was the guest evangelist in the church for the week, so he did not know her nor her older sister who stood close by. The older sister was encouraging her to relate something to Chappell, the nature of which was not immediately clear. Finally, after considerable coaxing, the little girl told that on the day before she had received a telephone call from a lady who was visiting in the city from out of state. The lady had dialed the wrong number. Although the little girl did not know who the lady was, she began to talk to her. Reaching to make conversation, as children often do, the girl remembered that there would be preaching at her church that evening so she passed along that bit of information and invited the lady to attend. The little girl, warming to her story as she told it, said, "The lady said she hadn't been inside a church in 20 years." Then, with excitement in her voice, the child said, "She was at church

86

tonight. I talked to her. And when you asked for people to accept Jesus, she was one of those who came forward.''

The lady was from out of state. She was in that particular city for a particular purpose and had her own agenda. To go into a strange church and hear a visiting evangelist preach was not a big item on her list of things to do. It was not a good time. But something about the little girl's invitation led her to take advantage of the opportunity. Probably a dozen reasons why she could not go raced through her mind: the circumstances were not right, she didn't have time; you can imagine the other reasons. At some point, however, it came to her that although things were not as she would have arranged them, it was an opportunity and she would seize it.

When you are waiting on the "right time" to come to Christ or if you are delaying your commitment until circumstances are "right," remember the woman in Luke's story who was so full of joy and gratitude that she would take advantage of any opportunity to praise God for what he had done for her through Christ Jesus her Lord! Those who are resolved will 'catch as catch can.' Those who have no resolve will never catch up to just the right opportunity. It will always be the wrong time.

The Attention

The gracious attention bestowed upon Jesus by the woman appears even greater when we take into account that the Pharisee-host had been remiss in extending the basic courtesies. William Barclay was told in one of his commentaries that when a guest entered the house in Bible times, three things were always done: the host gave the guest the kiss of peace; cool water was poured over the guest's feet; and either a pinch of incense was burned or a drop of ointment (or fragrance) was placed upon the head of the guest. These were not exceptional considerations, but common courtesies.

The Pharisee mumbles against the woman for what she had done and insinuates that Jesus is wasting his time and emotion on someone so undeserving. Jesus overheard his comments, which included the assertion that Jesus was not a prophet or else he would have known what kind of woman was fawning over him. Jesus then proceeds to point out what Simon, the host, had not done, but first he related a brief story:

> *"Simon, I have something to say to you.' And he answered, 'What is it Teacher?' 'A certain creditor had two debtors; one owed five hundred denarii, and the other fifty. When they could not pay, he forgave them both. Now which of them will love him more?' Simon answered, 'The one, I suppose, to whom he forgave more.' And he said to him, 'You have judged rightly' (Luke 7:40-43)."*

Having set up the lesson in the same manner which Nathan used with David, Jesus now catches Simon flat-footed:

> *"Then turning toward the woman he said to Simon, 'Do you see this woman? I entered your house, you gave me no water for my feet, but she has wet my feet with her tears and wiped them with her hair. You gave me no kiss, but from the time I came in she has not ceased to kiss my feet. You did not anoint my head with oil, but she has anointed my feet with ointment. Therefore I tell you, her sins, which are many, are forgiven, for she loved much; but he who is forgiven little, loves little.' And he said to her, 'Your sins are forgiven' (Luke 7:44-48)."*

If Simon had not been suspect in the beginning, he is now. Why had he invited Jesus into his home in the first place? There is the outside chance that he was a reluctant admirer, similar to Nicodemus, but his total lack of courtesy causes us to doubt that. Probably, he had invited Jesus out of sheer curiosity. Should Jesus be so novel as to be entertaining, or should he

88

disclose some information which could be used against him — all the better.

Jesus appears not to have been offended nearly so much by Simon's lack of courtesy as by his inability to comprehend the whole matter of forgiveness. He saw no need for forgiveness in his own life, for he had done nothing wrong. He saw no chance for forgiveness for the woman because she had done nothing right.

You and I are somewhere between Simon and the woman, inclined toward one extreme or the other. We either perceive Christ as something of a curiosity, showing him little or no serious regard, or we perceive him as Lord of our lives, someone to honor at every opportunity (no opportunity wasted) because we have been forgiven much!

The Pharisee and the woman show us both ends of the spectrum. Both were expressing their faith; that is to say, both were behaving in a manner indicative of their faith, indicative of their consciousness of being forgiven. We are there, at some point on the spectrum, enthusiastically expressing our faith, or blandly not expressing our faith, in response to forgiveness for our sins. If we have personally experienced forgiveness for our sins, then like the woman, we cannot praise God enough. If we have not had the experience, then like the Pharisee, we stand in the presence of praise and ask, "What is going on?"

Expression Of Faith

Faith, or more precisely, the expression of faith, is the primary focus of our text. Forgiveness is brought into the picture, but only to explain why the woman was expressing herself with such abandon. Jesus did not say "forgiveness has saved you," but rather, "Your faith has saved you." So the question is not, "Did she have faith?" She did. The question is not "What is faith?" That question is as broad as it is long. The letter to the Hebrews explains that faith means we are confident of what we hope for and convinced of what we do not see. John Dewey, seeking to be helpful, said, "Faith is the tendency toward action, the matrix of all formulated creed and the inspiration of endeavor." Walter Rathenau said, "Faith creates the mood in which events are determined." Do you begin to see why we do not wish to pursue a definition of faith. To do so would only tangle us up in our own feet. And clearly, the question is not, "Are there degrees of faith?" We yield our curiosity about this question to those folk who are inclined to ponder such things as "how many angels can dance on the point of a needle?" Jesus commended the woman for her faith. Rather than beat it to death, just sit back and enjoy seeing what it produced:

A Generous Attitude

If the woman had done only what she could afford to do, this story would not be in the Bible. She did not have the kind of income to allow her to be so lavish in her expressions. She did not have the kind of reputation that could modify a bizarre action. She had long since surrendered her reputation. Could she "afford" to do something now which would suggest that she had surrendered her sanity, too? Hardly. She could not "afford" another embarrassment any more than she could afford to "waste" a flask of precious ointment. Obviously, her faith delivered her at the speed of light beyond such selfish questions as, "How long could this ointment last me if I am careful with it," and "How much money could I get for this alabaster flask and ointment if I sold them?" Had she responded to Christ by doing what she could "afford" to do, we would never have heard of this woman!

To know and experience Christ is to want to love and honor Christ with the best that we have. Love does not count the costs or consider the limits. It just pours and pours itself out upon the beloved. How many sweethearts in love do you know

90

who keep an itemized list of expenses of what they have spent on each other? How many parents do you know who maintain a financial record against expenses involved in rearing their children, and then when the child becomes an adult, a reimbursement is demanded? For that matter, how many parents do you know who only do for their child what they can afford to do? Love does not bother to add up the column, because it doesn't bother to enter anything in the column. When we think of it in this way, and then think of the woman anointing Jesus, we begin to understand what Paul meant when he wrote, "Love never ends." I would not be surprised if the woman was not disapointed because she had only one flask of ointment to pour out. She probably would have emptied an entire vase if it had been available! Just be assured that the thought of what she could "afford" never entered her mind. Love is generous. Knowing this, I make it a point never to preach about money or how much a Christian ought to give as an expression of faith. If a person truly loves Christ, their expression of faith will reflect it.

Jesus commended the woman for her faith. Her generous attitude was a product of that faith.

A Worshipful Attitude

By anointing Jesus, the woman was actually making a praise offering. It was in her heart to praise, honor, and adore the one who had transformed her life, and one of the wonderful things about praise, honor, and adoration is that all three are directed beyond oneself. The worshipful attitude focuses upon something higher than personal regard, taking no thought of any advantage which might be gained. That is to say, worshiping God in order to gain any possible spiritual leverage, "Doing this for God in order to make it easier for God to do this for me." That is a sorry motivation, isn't it? Such an attitude is not produced by faith, but by a selfish, mercenary mind. Praise and adoration issue freely from a mind that is saturated with the desire to give. Worship involves acts of praise; something that a selfish mind is incapable of rendering. The adoring mind cannot render enough. There is no need to ask, "Of which mind was the woman?" There is the need to ask, "Of what mind are we?" remembering that faith produces a worshipful attitude.

Confident Attitude

We should not miss the attitude in which the woman entered the Pharisee's home. Although uninvited, she made no apology. Kneeling at the feet of Jesus, she made no explanation. For her reputation, she made no excuses. Filled with emotion, she made no pretense. As a matter of fact, there is no record that she ever said anything. Confident in faith, and taking no notice of anyone or anything except the one she had come to praise, she proceeded.

Faith produces confidence. Someone has told about a woman who became a Christian late in life. The deep lines in her face and dark places beneath her eyes reflected the kind of life she had lived. But, like the thief on the cross and the laborers who came late to the vineyard, she couldn't turn the clock back and start at the beginning, so she would do the next best thing: come to Christ and start from there. It was not easy. Her old friends ridiculed her and complained that her new lifestyle made them uncomfortable. Finally, one of them hatefully snapped at her; "Who do you think you are anyway, so high and mighty all of a sudden? You're nothing but an ugly old woman!" To which the woman (like the woman of our text) made no apology, explanation, excuse, nor pretense. She only smiled confidently and replied, "Yes, but isn't it wonderful that God can love an ugly, old woman like me?"

There is no substitute for the confidence produced by faith.

There was ointment. It was precious. There were tears. They were precious, too. Mingling together on the feet of Jesus, they were the very best that she could give. Truly an "outward" and "inward" expression of faith!

What now about your own expression of faith? If it were to be publicly called into account, would it be more than you could "afford" or more than you could afford to say?

"To Be Or Not To Be" ... Is NOT The Question

"They" say that the next President of the United States is going to be a woman. "They" say that the next winter will be one of the coldest on record. "They" say that two heads are better than one. "They" say that if a rooster crows late in the day, rain is on the way.

Surely you have heard of "They." It is almost certain that at one time or another you have referred to "They" when relating some bit of information in the course of a conversation. "They" say! "They" are always saying something. And it is not enough that they are always saying something, "They" are always doing something. "They are wearing a lot of browns and blues together this year." "They are really catching fish on Lake _____, about 10 feet away from the bank, using crickets for bait." "They are wearing such-and-such jogging shoes now."

Who composes this faceless, all-knowing, oft-quoted body of experts on virtually every subject?

It is not really necessary to reach for their names or strain to see their faces. Regardless of who they are or what they look like, we know that "They" exert a tremendous influence upon what we say and do. "They" have a great deal to do with the shaping of public opinion. As a matter of fact, "They" may sometimes be public opinion.

When Jesus and his disciples had come to Bethsaida, they sought out a place to pray privately. At some point during their prayers, Jesus abruptly asked, "Who do they say that I am?" Perhaps he was seeking to confirm what he himself had, overheard or asking for information about something he had been unable to determine, or seeking an opportunity to challenge the disciples to clarify and formalize their own commitment. Judging from the nature of the dialogue, I suspect it was the latter alternative.

"Who do they say that I am?" Jesus asked. The disciples replied, "They are saying that you are John the Baptist. They are also saying that you are Elijah come back to life and, if not Elijah, then one of the other prophets." Clearly, he was generating some discussion among the people. He was not being ignored. He was not being referred to as a mad-man or a here-today-gone-tomorrow sensationalist. But you will observe, neither were "They" saying anything about his being the Son of God. The thought apparently had not occurred to them. Similarities between Jesus and prophetic figures of the past were easily drawn. The disciples replied to Jesus' question on the basis of what they had heard and observed. "(They) are saying that you are John the Baptist, or Elijah, or one of the prophets."

Jesus pressed the matter further. "But who do you say that I am?"

What a totally disarming question! No more reporting popular comments. No more monitoring of public opinion. No more repetition of common knowledge. The time had come for personal conviction to be said out loud. Jesus needed to hear the disciples express it. The disciples needed to hear themselves express it. The light was now turned up to maximum intensity, not upon "They," but upon the disciples personally. "Who do you say that I am?"

It inevitably comes down to that, doesn't it? It is one thing to be able to quote theologians; it is another to be in possession of a theology. To know the ruminations of Paul Tillich, Karl Barth, Soren Kierkegaard, and other religious thinkers, adds to knowledge. But to know the love of God, the grace of the Lord Jesus Christ, and the abiding presence of the Holy Spirit, adds to faith. "Who do you say that I am?" Jesus asked. That is the question.

Several years ago, a minister friend and I engaged in a good-natured exchange of theological opinions. The two of us were enrolled in seminary at the time and most anxious to articulate personal beliefs in the words of our newly acquired vocabularies. The great dialogue was taking place in my friend's apartment and well within earshot of his wife, who stood at the kitchen sink up to her elbows in dishwater. The specific topic of the lively discussion has long since faded from memory, but I do recall that both of us claimed the victory. To confirm the matter one way or the other, my friend brought his wife into it. "What do you believe, dear?" Although 25 years have passed since she made the reply, the words remain clearly in my mind; "I don't really know who is right, but what Larry is saying sounds more like what mother and daddy believe than what you say."

The question was not, "What do your parents believe?" but "What do you believe?" The reply was a classical "They say" response. It is always easier to repeat than to think, isn't it?

Christian friends, you and I have studied the Bible. We have read and listened to other people's beliefs concerning Christ. We know what John Wesley believed. We know what Billy Graham believes. We know what commentaries and a host of Christian writers relate about belief. We know what televangelists believe and what some wise old sages in our local churches are convinced of. We know what our parents, relatives, and friends believe about Christ. We know what "They" all say. As a matter of fact, we do an admirable job of repeating what "They" say, especially if it serves us well in a conversation or may be offered in reply to a direct question in such a way that enables us to dodge expressing a personal opinion. "They say" is such a handy thing to say. But the unavoidable question, posed by the eternal Christ, is always the same: "Who do you say that I am?" That is the question.

Think now, before answering.

(1) Do not claim Jesus as Lord while continuing to be bound to a temporal attitude about possessions. One cancels out the other. One has to do with possessing. The other has to do with being possessed.

Peculiar notions about temporal things surface from time to time. Several years ago, my wife and I visited relatives in Jefferson City, Missouri. We both love to browse in little out-of-the-way shops, especially rummage and junktique stores. We were delighted to find a small building on one of the main streets, literally crammed full of almost every kind of old, used article imaginable. Hundreds of objects were tightly stuffed against the inside of the large storefront window, floor to ceiling. The front door was opened but piled full of merchandise. As unbelievable as it may seem, there was no possible way to enter the building by the front door. Solid — top to bottom — solid assorted collectibles. Until that time, I had not seen, nor have I since seen, a space with every single inch so totally stuffed with "stuff." It was amazing. An old fellow leaned back in a cane bottomed chair against the outside wall, picking his teeth. He watched us with interest as we peered through the large window and commented about the tremendous volume of what-nots. I spied an old stone jug in the midst of the hundreds of things pressed against the inside of the window. With a mind to buy the jug, I asked the old gentleman if he was the proprietor. "I am," he admitted. "How much for that stone jug?" I asked, pointing toward it. "It ain't for sale," he replied. Somewhat confused, I asked why it was not for sale. "I can't get to it," he said. "Well, do you think I could get to it?" I asked. "Nope," he countered, "and even if you could, it ain't for sale. I don't want to sell it."

Strange, I thought, that a man should operate a place of business and then refuse to do business. We later discovered from local merchants that the man hasn't sold anything in a long time. He just goes down every morning, opens the front door, leans back in his chair on the sidewalk, and about 4 p.m., locks up and goes home. He can't sell anything because he can't get to it. Even if he could get to it, he is too attached to it to sell it. It is his "stuff." He has become so fond of his inventory that he cannot bear to part with it. "Things" have a way of doing that to a person, crowding out everything else, accumulating to the point of excess, and becoming too dear to part with.

The rich young man described in Mark 10:17-22 fell on his knees before Jesus and asked, "Good Teacher, what must I do to inherit eternal life?" We take notice of the fact that the young man did not inquire about how to get closer to God or how to be saved, or how to honor Christ. He was interested in eternal life, something else he could acquire. It is ironic that if he had asked how to embrace the will of God in his life, Jesus could have spoken to him of peace and security. Instead, Jesus' reply caused him great distress; ". . . sell what you have and give it to the poor, and you will have treasures in heaven; and come, follow me." The man was devastated. The Scriptures say, "his countenance fell, and he went away sorrowful; for he had great possessions (Mark 10:22)." Like the old man with his rummage, he had become too attached to his "stuff."

So now, what about your things? We have smiled at the man with his rummage, and felt pity for the rich young ruler, but what about your things? I don't know what they are; a family heirloom; your first dollar, a pocket knife you've had for years, a lucky charm, a string of beads with special meaning, the automobile that you park all by itself at the other end of the parking lot so no one will open their car door against it? You have your things. That's all right, so long as they don't crowd out everything else, accumulate to the point of excess, or become too dear to part with.

We cannot be bound to Christ while continuing to be bound to a temporal attitude about possessions. One cancels out the other.

"Who do you say that I am?" That is the question. Think again before answering.

(2) Do not claim Jesus as Lord while continuing to look at people and the world through the wrong end of a telescope. On September 12, 1989, President Bush appealed in a live television broadcast to millions of schoolchildren to reject drugs. The 15-minute broadcast was carried live by the four major television networks as well as educational cable systems. A reporter from the *Arkansas Gazette* sat with students and

viewed the message at one of the junior high schools in Little Rock. Following the telecast, the reporter interviewed several students selected at random. The students were unimpressed with the president's message. "I sat on the porch and watched two drug busts over the weekend," said a ninth grader. "My aunt was on 'crack' and she had a son and they can't feed him properly," said an eighth grader. Another student added that one of her friends was presently hospitalized with convulsions after a drug overdose, and her cousin tried to fly out a window after taking "angel dust." The junior high students felt they know a great deal more about drugs than the President of the United States.

On September 13, the day after the president's message, as a part of his declared war on drugs, the Pentagon complained that the war on drugs was diverting too many dollars from the defense program! In a lengthy Associated Press article, Pentagon officials criticized the proposal of one of our U. S. senators that a modest portion of military money be directed to increased anti-drug efforts.

In heaven's name! Our children are wading around now in the quagmire of a vast drug culture, popping pills, sniffing stuff up their noses and injecting things into their veins which you and I can't even pronounce, and the Pentagon is more interested in underwriting the manufacture of some exotic destructive machines which will be obsolete before they are taken off the blocks. Somebody is viewing people and the world through the wrong end of a telescope.

On the lighter side, the same phenomenon sometimes surfaces in more subtle, less harmful ways. Having attended morning worship at their church, the man and his wife were on their way home. "Henry," said she, "did you see that man five or six pews in front of us with that awful cow-lick in his hair?" Henry had taken no notice of the cow-lick. "Well, did you see all the plaster flaking off the ceiling right over your head?" Henry looked a little surprised and said, "No, I failed to notice that." They had not gone far when the wife thought of something else. "Henry, did you hear the woman in the choir

bellowing like a calf, trying to be heard above everybody else?"
"No," replied Henry, "Which one was she?" The wife rolled
her shoulders and sighed, "Well, you couldn't miss seeing the
long thread hanging from the hem of the minister's robe."
"Sorry dear," said Henry, "I guess I was trying to listen to
the sermon and missed all that other business." The little
woman then observed, "Henry, sometimes I think it doesn't
do you a bit of good to go to church!"

Sometimes it is serious. Sometimes, it is not so serious. But
then, sometimes we find ourselves looking at people and the
world through the wrong end of a telescope.

If your eye is fixed upon Christ Jesus, then all else comes
into proper focus and perspective. The Scripture reads, "If
thine eyes be single, thy whole body shall be full of light (Matthew 6:22 KJV)."

Jesus Christ cannot be Lord and things be out of focus.
One cancels out the other.

"Who do you say that I am?" That is the question.

Think one last time before answering.

(3) Do not claim Jesus as Lord while clinging to some false
security. Norman Vincent Peale has observed, "It is curious
and sad the way much of the intellectual climate has changed.
Once we roared like lions for liberty; now we bleat like sheep
for security." In the absence of security, confidence and a sense
of well-being go begging. We have a low tolerance for insecurity. Frankly, there is only one thing worse than insecurity and
that is false security, especially if one is not even aware that
it is a false security.

In the little community where I was raised, there lived a
wise old school teacher named Henrietta Gill. Mrs. Gill lived
just across the alley directly behind our house. She wore her
grey hair up in a bun, drove a black model-T Ford, and always displayed a countenance indicative of a person who knew
most everything there was to know. She did know things —
so many things that she was considered the sage of Craighead
County. One of Mrs. Gill's wise pronouncements was that our
town would never experience a severe storm. It was common

knowledge that the county had never experienced a severe storm, so everyone just assumed that the time honored pronouncement was correct. Let me tell you something about security here. When we played ball in the street as children and the summer sky became cloudy, not one time did we expect anything but rain of unpredictable duration. No high wind, window-rattling thunder, or slashing lightning to rip, blast, or demolish. The thought was simply not in our minds. We simply waited out the weather and wrote it off as interruption.

In 1967, a killer tornado ripped through my hometown, thrashing an unbelievable swath, claiming the lives of 32 persons. The school I had attended, four houses down from my home, was demolished. The big trees in my parents' yard had been twisted like wet paper towels. Widespread destruction beyond description had not only devastated the little town and miles of rural surroundings, it had rendered everyone in the area incredibly limp; bewildered. Not only were homes, property, fields, woods, businesses, and lives destroyed, but our "security" was brutally shattered. It was difficult to gather in the tornado's absolute annihilation of the area. It was difficult to gather in that Mrs. Gill had been wrong. It was, now, even more difficult to gather in how we could have been naive enough to have assumed such a false security in the first place.

Some of you know what it is to have your securities shattered. And they have all proven to be false, haven't they? Some of the others of you are still riding high on the crest of your "securities" and don't know what this is about. It doesn't matter; all our false securities will eventually become conspicuous by their absence. Exercise programs, low-calorie diets, financial investments, finely laid plans for the future — all good things to do, but don't flatter them by referring to them as "securities." One potent storm in your life can erase your good health, empty your savings account, or dramatically alter the direction of your future; perhaps all three at the same time!

If it is security you want, listen to this:

"God is my shield and the horn of my salvation, my high tower and my refuge (2 Samuel 22:3)."

"God is our refuge and strength, a very present help in trouble (Psalm 46:1)."

"Therefore, do not be anxious, saying, 'What shall we eat?' or 'What shall we drink?' or 'What shall we wear?' . . . But seek first his kingdom and his righteousness and all these things shall be yours as well (Matthew 6:31-33)."

Do not claim Christ as Lord while continuing to be bound to a temporal attitude about possessions, continuing to look at people and the world through the wrong end of a telescope, or clinging to some false security.

Think now. The question will not go away; "Who do you say that I am?"

How do you answer now?

The Set Face And The Turned Head

"I know you've been sworn in and I've read your complaint." So begins Judge Wapner as another case unfolds on the popular television series, "People's Court." Repeating the phrase before each case, the implication is that the litigants have already placed their hands on the Bible and sworn to tell nothing "but the truth." However, courtroom cases do not progress far until it becomes apparent that either the plaintiff or the defendant is lying. Immediately, the whole matter of swearing-in comes into question. What good did it really do if one, or both parties involved knew from the beginning that they would not hesitate to bend the facts around to fit their own purposes? Beneath the long look, it appears that the swearing-in has become nothing more than a formality to be hurdled in order to get on with the business at hand. Very much, I suppose, like some meetings we attend and someone asks someone else to "open with a prayer." The prayer signals the formal "opening" of the meeting and it has been my experience that the mood and content of such meetings are usually what they would have been whether the prayer was prayed or not. It does appear from time to time that God receives a tip of the hat and then we move on to deal with the business at hand.

Committing oneself to tell the truth, committing a meeting to the fulfillment of God's will, or committing one's behavior to the glory of God; all of these are noble and highly commendable. However, if all we are committed to is the formality of making the commitment, we are, as someone expressed it, "a bluster, a bluff, an empty show."

A good case could be made for the claim that our generation is the perfect example of what happens when commitments are neutralized or largely ignored. Can you think of another time in history when the "everyone for himself, grab-what-you-can-now, get out of my way" attitude has been more prevalent? We are dangerously close to the point of becoming a people committed to the unencumbered pursuit of whatever it is we are trying to pursue. More and more we are witnesses to behavior which reflects a disturbing point of view; "Don't ask permission; just use it, take it, do it!"

Not long ago, I was driving through a neighborhood on my way home and came to a stop behind two other cars at a stop sign. The car immediately in front of me was occupied by a middle-aged lady. The car in front of her was a red convertible occupied by two teenagers. Although there was no other traffic in sight, the convertible did not proceed. The occupants were leisurely adjusting the tape player, smoothing their hair, and carrying on a conversation as if they were on private property instead of a public street. After a while, the lady in the middle car, apparently thinking the youngsters were not aware that they could proceed, tapped the horn lightly. At that, the passenger in the convertible stood up in the front seat, turned around to stare hatefully at the woman, shouted obscenities and made numerous vulgar gestures. When the car finally did proceed, it did so at a slow, mocking speed with the driver turning around to punctuate the insult by adding additional gestures. I am relatively certain that the lady wished she had never touched the horn. As it happened, we all continued in the same direction and sure enough, found ourselves at another stop sign. The only difference this time was the lady received the same treatment without sounding the horn. Having made their point, the red convertible roared away with tires squealing and the tape player blasting. Mercifully, it screeched around a corner and disappeared. I was reminded of a bumper sticker I saw once which read, "If you don't like the way I drive, stay off the sidewalk." Except the attitude exhibited in this case seems to have been, "If you don't like the fact that you don't matter in my opinion, don't bother me about it.''

The two people in the red convertible just happened to be teenagers and were by no means representative of all teens. We all know that adults can be equally obnoxious. This is not an observation about a particular age group, but about a specific attitude. The attitude which says, "Get out of my way!" The attitude which, if it is committed at all, is committed to the unencumbered pursuit of whatever is being pursued.

Let us look now at this whole matter of commitment and how it applies to a generation in which commitment itself has become neutralized. More importantly, we all want to prayerfully determine the nature of commitment as it pertains to the way of Christ.

We are told twice in the opening of our text that Jesus' face was "set toward Jerusalem." Jerusalem, Jerusalem alone, was his destination. He had business there. He was determined to arrive because he had a purpose larger than his own agenda. En route, an unnamed man approaches Jesus on a country road and declares a verbal commitment, "I will follow you wherever you go." From all appearances, a verbal commitment was all it was because the man is never mentioned again. Farther down the road, Jesus invites another man to follow him. The man responded by saying that he first had to go bury his father. As harsh as this may seem, he was committed to something else and would not commit to Christ despite Jesus' instruction to "Let the dead bury the dead." Soon afterwards, yet another man said to Jesus, "I will follow you, Lord, but let me first say farewell to those at my home." In other words, he "set his face" toward Christ but turned his head toward home. Jesus replied, "No one who puts his hand to the plow and looks back is fit for the kingdom of God." It is not that Jesus was impatient or did not have time to wait. It was simply a matter of if the man had reservations on the front end of commitment, what would happen when the going got really tough?

Our text, in its entirety, is about commitment and/or the lack of it. It is about Jesus "setting l.is face" and three men "turning their heads."

Three words come to mind as being descriptive of the kind of commitment to which the gospel invites us.

The first word is "total."

Following his baptism, our Lord was led by the Spirit to a desolate, solitary place where he encountered severe temptations. Be sure of this one thing; they were genuine temptations in every sense of the word, or else the Scriptures would have found a way around saying, "Jesus was led up by the Spirit into the wilderness to be tempted by the devil (Matthew 4:1)." The temptations were intense. He was tempted to: turn stones into bread (provide for his physical needs); throw himself from the pinnacle of the temple (resort to sensationalism); and bow down and worship Satan (compromise and conform). Anyone who suggests that Jesus' divinity precluded the possibility of any of these being real options, simply holds the Scriptures to be in error. Of a truth, our Lord was thrown into the crucible of determining his commitment. Inclinations and partial allegiances would have been convenient options, but they were not in our Lord's mind. When he emerged from the temptations, there were no reservations about what he was going to do. The program was clear and he was totally committed to it. The will of God was paramount and he was totally dedicated to it. The reconciliation of all creation was the objective and, although it would require the supreme sacrifice, he was totally committed to it. Please take notice that this is the kind of commitment to which the gospel invites us. Total commitment. Even as the ministry of Christ was not begun or fulfilled on the reluctant embrace of half-hearted resolve, neither can we embrace the way of Christ and surrender ourselves unto the will of God with anything less than unreserved commitment.

Nicodemus is a familiar Bible name to us because he has been so frequently referred to as a bad example. There is every possibility that the church through the centuries has been unkind to Nicodemus, but there is precious little in the gospel story to redeem him. It is told that he came to Jesus secretly by night, uttered a faint, timid remark in defense of Jesus, and assisted Joseph of Arimathea in preparing the body of Jesus for burial. He never declared openly as a follower of Christ and then when it was too late, he came around wanting to do a good work. The man bothers us because there is such about him that mirrors some of our own inclinations to be committed to being uncommitted.

It is told that a missionary preached in a remote, poverty ridden area in west Africa. He appealed for support of Christian work throughout the area and encouraged those present to give what they could toward the construction of a building which would serve as a medical clinic and a place of worship. Approximately two hours after the worship service, a young woman came to the missionary and presented him with $40 to be used for the building project. The missionary was stunned. Where on earth could that woman come up with such a large sum of money in a region afflicted by painfully forbidding circumstances? Confounded, he posed this question as politely as he knew how to the young woman. He was informed that after hearing the missionary preach about Jesus and being challenged to do something for Jesus, and having nothing to give, she had gone to a wealthy planter and sold herself into his service for the rest of her life. Let us be clear about what I have just told you. She had sold herself into the service of the landowner; she had given herself into the service of Jesus Christ. Not partially, but totally. That sounds like a radical price to pay doesn't it? However, if you think such a measure of commitment is radical, read again the words of our text and be impressed that the lifetime commitment is exactly what is called for. A lifetime of service. Call it anything you please, but do not call it less than it is; total commitment. Nicodemus could not handle it. The three unnamed men in our text could not deal with it. Can you and I deal with it?

The second word descriptive of the kind of commitment to which the gospel invites us is "tenacious."

Sam Jones once remarked that a woman can go into a store containing $1 million worth of inventory, buy a card of needles and leave without buying anything else. How? Because the only thing she had on her mind was a card of needles. One purpose, a solitary mission, or to use a scriptural phrase, "singleness of eye." That is half the matter. Add to that the persistent, relentless pursuit of the object and you have commitment sealed with tenacity. To use a very unscriptural untheological word, the kind of commitment we see demonstrated in the Scriptures brings to mind the word, "flypaper." Would you agree that flypaper tends to cling like a magnet to that with which it comes in contact? If you think flypaper is tenacious, let me read you something:

> *"Five times I have received at the hands of the Jews the forty lashes less one. Three times I have been beaten with rods; once I was stoned. Three times I have been shipwrecked; a night and a day I have been adrift at sea; on frequent journeys; in danger from rivers, dangers from robbers, dangers from my own people, danger from Gentiles, danger in the city, danger in the wilderness, danger at sea, danger from false brethren; in toil and hardship, through many a sleepless night, in hunger and thirst, often without food, in cold and exposure. And apart from other things, there is the daily pressure upon me of my anxiety for all the churches (2 Corinthians 11:24-28)."*

Compared to Paul, flypaper is a lesser example of tenacity. However, compared to Paul, our own commitment might be described as "flyweight."

We are referring now to the commitment which gets on a trail and stays on it. It does not grow weary nor it is distracted. A statewide hunger rally was held on the campus of one of our colleges in the late '70s. Hundreds of sensitive, concerned, well-meaning church leaders filled the auditorium to listen to staggering statistics about the effects of world hunger and view frame after frame of a slide presentation showing under-nourished, skeletal-like figures covered with insects. The program was graphic, emotional, and presented quite effectively. Unfortunately, the presentation ran a little longer than expected and, about ten minutes past noon, the motion was made that we adjourn for lunch. People were hungry. Further proceedings of the hunger rally were scheduled around the noon meal rather than everyone foregoing the meal and contributing what we would have paid for the meal to world hunger. It is sad to tell, but we could not even get on the trail of the program, much less stay on the trail toward productive response. The only exhibition of tenacity related to a commitment in this instance was the stubborn insistence to maintain our own feeding schedule. The nature of true commitment was illustrated well enough, but the object was in contradiction to the lesson.

Who is that walking yonder in the shadows? It looks like — yes, it is Nicodemus. He discovers the trail, it mingles in his senses, it stirs him to want to go on. He is on the trail. No, now he is off. He crosses it again but he is not after the prize. He is only curious about the nature of the trail. He is not committed to the trail, much less him to whom the trail leads. The Scriptures depict him as showing up on the trail from time to time, but he cannot stay on it.

There is another figure. He is walking away from us, but it looks like — yes, it is Demas. We remember Demas. He was on the trail at Colossae but according to Paul's letter to Timothy, "Demas has deserted me in love with the present world (2 Timothy 4:10)." He lost the trail.

Have you lost the trail or are you clinging to it tenaciously? Is your commitment like "flypaper" or is it "fly-weight?"

The last word I want to suggest to you as being descriptive of the kind of commitment to which the gospel invites us is "translated."

Do you know what a midnight confession is? That is when you wake up late at night or in the wee hours of the morning and your mind is tormented by something and, whatever it is, you can't sleep. It is something you need to put right, or resolve, or do whatever it takes to eliminate the misery. In desperate cases (and in the quiet darkness surrounding you when you ought to be asleep, things have a way of being desperate) you pray, "Dear Lord, just help me to solve this thing and I will . . ." I do not know how you fill in that blank, but you do. Or, we wake up at night experiencing excruciating pain between our hip and waistline. "Oh God, I don't want to have a kidney stone tonight. If you will just deliver me from this situation and let it just be a muscle spasm, I will . . ." (if you have ever had a kidney stone, you will pray this prayer).

What noble, far-reaching promises we made to God in midnight confessions. We rededicate our lives to Christ, increase our tithe, volunteer for church work, vow to be more civil to our spouse and children, and on and on. Then, comes daylight, and things are not nearly as desperate as we had supposed and our midnight confessions blend in with the morning mist and are chased away by the sun.

My friends, your commitment and my commitment are not worth the breath they are muttered with unless they can be translated into the light of day. A commitment that is as good in daylight as in darkness is the kind of commitment we are reaching for.

Nicodemus perhaps made a midnight resolve, "coming by night," but it could not stand up in the light of day. He was unable to translate his good intentions from the shadows into daylight devotion.

Is your commitment, regardless as to when it was assumed — day or night — translatable into service?

Yes, a good case could be made for the claim that our generation is the perfect example of what happens when commitments are neutralized. The Christian faith invites us not to internalize Christ and a commitment to him, totally, tenaciously and translating that which we have embraced into service.

Fleshing Out The Word

In the summer of 1983, I participated in a ministerial exchange program sponsored by my denomination. My assignment was to a circuit of churches on the Isle of Man, a tiny island located in the Irish Sea. The months preceding the exchange included considerable correspondence with the minister on the island with whom I would exchange pastoral duties for six weeks. Additionally, there were all kinds of other preparations to be seen after: passports, financial arrangements, reading everything available about the Isle of Man, and trying to anticipate everything which could go wrong (on both sides of the ocean) and allow for it. Despite all that, the Isle of Man was still pretty much just a place on the map to me and, for some reason, the whole business of the exchange simply had not come alive for me. That is, until the week before we were to leave.

A wonderful couple in our church invited my wife and me to have dinner with them one evening in their home. Knowing that our main meat dish for the next six weeks was to be lamb, they served lamb and sauce to acquaint us with a food unfamiliar to our palates. But the really special thing they did was to invite another guest, a Presbyterian minister friend, originally from Scotland. Enjoyment of the meal was exceeded only by our fascination with the good brother's spell-binding dialect. We all asked questions just to hear him speak. Following the meal, he referred to a world map, pointing out his birthplace, the birthplace of Robert Burns and other famous Scots, commented about St. Giles Cathedral, the Edinburg Castle, Waverly Station, and "Just here," he said, "not many miles from Scotland, is the Isle of Man where ye will soon be and I have been many times."

It all came alive for me then. It came alive for me because a "real person" representing a wonderful reality, an "eyewitness," had fleshed-out, actualized something beyond my experience.

There is no better witness than an eyewitness. There is no better example than a living example. Jesus knew that when he "appointed 70 others, and sent them on ahead of him, two by two, into every town and place where he himself was about to come (Luke 10:1)."

God teaches us in his word, in just such examples as our text, of the dynamic, creative, interpretive power of the personality.

God conceived a design in his great mind for creation. That design was willed into actuality. However, God was still lonely. Creation was incomplete somehow. How did he address this loneliness? Fashion a prototype for a harmonic cosmic structure, divine a great idea, assemble a computer, construct a robot, or design a dynamic program? The missing ingredient, the key part, the thing which was to bind it all together, was added: "Male and female created he them." Let us stop talking around the word and say it: persons!

It cannot be emphasized enough that of all things in the universe, the hinge article, the thing with which the Spirit of God does business, the thing which shall cause the total plan of God to work (or not work) is persons.

Oh yes, some other things are well designed, ingeniously made, but they are not supremely pivotal.

• **Instinct.** We have all read and pondered about the swallows which annually make their way back to Capistrano. We know that when it is winter in California the swallows are in South America. Then, following the winter, they return to California. As a matter of fact, they return on the same day each year — March 19. It is documented that, despite the 6,000 mile journey, they have regularly returned on this date except in 1935 when they were delayed by storms. To be sure, there is a controlling, powerful force innate to the animal kingdom — instinct — but it is not supremely pivotal to the fulfillment of God's plan.

114

• **Tradition.** No one would question that tradition is an influential factor upon any social setting, but to claim that it is the epoxy which binds a community or area together is questionable. Especially since some of our revered traditions are considerably distorted in the first place. For example, we in the South have a tradition of enjoying an emotional involvement with the song, "Dixie." Many in the South regard it as "our song," or a kind of regional anthem. To sing of cotton and frosty mornings and living and dying for Dixie stirs up emotions which transport the mind back to an antebellum, magnolia shaded, honeysuckle scented nostalgia-plated era. How easy it is to picture in one's mind a pensive romantic sitting on a long ago veranda, peering across dew-covered gardenias and endless rows of cotton, lovingly writing down the words to "Dixie."

There is only one thing wrong with all that. It just isn't so. The song was written in 1854 by a man named Emmett, a member of a minstrel company. It was written as a "walk around" number to allow characters to change positions on stage and was first performed in New York City.

Tradition, distortions and all, exerts a strong influence but it is not supremely pivotal to the fulfillment of God's plan.

• **Great Ideas and Great Books.** Enough great ideas have been advanced through the centuries to change the world several times over. But great ideas, soon or late, invariably are outdistanced by other ideas perceived to be greater. Billions of books written as testaments to great ideas create an impressive bulk of material, but they are not supremely pivotal to the fulfillment of God's plan.

Clearly, all things in creation, celestial and terrestrial, the key to the fulfillment of God's plan is persons motivated by the Holy Spirit.

There is no better example than a living example! Several years ago, the Sears-Roebuck Company decided to merchandise a particular image. The image was one of youth, vitality, freshness, happiness, and all-American wholesomeness. That was the concept, and when Sears-Roebuck chose to portray the concept in a person, they selected Cheryl Tiegs. She was the personification of the idea. In the same manner, Norman Lear undertook to portray a certain element in America to convey, what was at the time, a rather daring social message. His new television series centered around a narrow minded bigot. The character? Archie Bunker.

When an idea or concept gets into a person, it comes alive! And again, there is no better example than a living example. Allow this Scripture to become fixed in your mind: "The Lord appointed 70 others and sent them on ahead of him, two by two, into every town and place where he himself was about to come." Forerunners of one who was to come, but also living examples of an idea; proof of a reality.

Let us now transpose some implications of our text to Christians in general.

(1) The Christian as forerunner. A forerunner prepares the way for one who is to come. John the Baptist clarified his own role and witness when he declared that he was preparing the way for the coming of one mightier than he. He was not the one of whom the Scriptures spoke, but he was important to the one of whom the Scriptures spoke, soon to come.

The Billy Graham Crusade came to Little Rock this past September. Besides being spiritually rewarding, it was quite impressive strictly because of the manner in which organizational details were carried out. Night after night, things moved along without the slightest hitch, so far as one could tell. Vehicles moved smoothly upon city streets, parking was uncomplicated and orderly. Getting in and out of the stadium was remarkably simple. Seating was casual and made easy by polite, easily identifiable ushers. The worship services themselves included a massive volunteer choir, excellent special music, well and effective personal witnesses, challenging sermons by Dr. Graham, and the invitation to respond to the leadership of the Spirit. Counselors were available for those who chose to respond, there was follow-up on new converts, and local pastors were notified for weeks following the crusade about individuals who had indicated a religious preference. The Billy

Graham Crusade accomplished a great work for the kingdom of God. But underline this one thing: without long months of preparation by the crusade team who had come as forerunners, the record would read quite differently. Having met with the team, I can confirm that they were excellent representatives for what they were promoting, proficient at what they were about, and assumed a tremendous personal responsibility for the success or failure of the mission.

Because we have named the name of Christ, you and I are forerunners of the coming kingdom. We pray for the grace to be good representatives of what we proclaim, proficient in our witness, and assume a personal ownership in the ultimate victory.

(2) The Christian as the Word became flesh. The gospel according to Luke relates how Jesus came to Nazareth, his home town, and attended the synagogue on the sabbath. Reading from the scroll, he quoted a passage from the prophet Isaiah; the Spirit of the Lord is upon me because he has anointed me to preach the good news to the poor . . . to proclaim the acceptable year of the Lord (Luke 4:18, 19)." When he had finished reading, he gave the scroll to an attendant and boldly announced, "This day this Scripture has been fulfilled in your hearing." Please observe that those present took no offense at this announcement. It was when Jesus proceeded beyond the claim of being the Word become flesh and began behaving as the personification of God's Word that they became upset. The concept had not disturbed them. The fleshing-out of the concept did (see 4:29). Fleshing-out, or living-out a concept — personifying something — inevitably brings consequences. The living example takes his or her chances, and that is precisely what the gospel invites us to do while assuring us that the matter of "risk" never comes into the consciousness which has been absorbed into the Spirit of God. Witness becomes a natural expression rather than a calculated risk.

About a month ago, I preached a series of sermons in a small church located in a lovely rural setting, far removed from the rush of traffic and the busy schedules of urban life. It was refreshing just to be in such a place, and even more uplifting to worship with such wonderful people. You know the kind of little country church I'm talking about. Many of us grew up worshiping in churches like them and most every pastor has served in such a church at one time or another. One of the first things I noticed upon entering the small sanctuary was a rather large wallhanging directly behind the pulpit. It was, I believe, what is referred to as a handmade "latch hook" portraying the last supper. I was impressed by its appearance, unusual size, and by the thousands of pushes and pulls of a needle required to create such a work. Having commented about it during the sermon, I was pleased, following the service, to meet the lady who had created it. Standing close to her husband, she smiled, "I am the lady who made the picture." I immediately observed that her vision was extremely poor. "I am sure it must have required a great deal of time," I replied. "Yes sir, it did," she sighed, "and I couldn't have done it without my husband. He had to describe all the colors of thread to me because my eyes are so bad I couldn't tell one from the other."

That was her witness. Actually, it was their witness — one stitch at a time: his eyes, her hands. Fleshing-out the Word.

Attending the services each evening was a little girl, whom I judged to be 10 or 11 years of age. She will always be in my memory. Badly crippled, feet pointed in, totally blind. One evening, her mother assisted her to the front of the church and into the pulpit area. "Step up," the mother whispered a couple of times. "Here's a step. Careful. All right, here's the microphone; hold it tight." A tape containing the musical accompaniment was inserted into a tape player and the little girl sang. The name of the song was, "She's Got Her Father's Eyes." When she finished, we all applauded. She was so happy that she applauded. For those of us in that place, the Word had become flesh.

If any of you think that you are not equipped to "flesh-out" the gospel, I invite you to come with me to a little country church and meet a little disabled girl and a woman almost blind who would be thrilled to have the equipment you have for witness. The Word becomes flesh when it becomes personified in you!

(3) The Christian as victorious. Jesus did not send the 70 out to fail. As a matter of fact, he instructed them not to waste much time or emotion on persons who were not receptive to their witness: "But whenever you enter a town and they do not receive you, go into its streets and say, 'Even the dust of your town that clings to our feet, we wipe off against you; nevertheless know this, that the kingdom of God has come near' (Luke 10:10, 11)." It was almost as if he was saying, "Don't even give failure the opportunity to happen. Press on toward the victory!" Jesus did not intend for his forerunners, or witnesses, to have their spirits sapped by being rejected when there were so many positive opportunities to be claimed for the kingdom. And when they returned, they "returned with joy, saying, 'Lord, even the demons are subject to us in your name' (Luke 10:18)."

Do not mistake the work and ministry of Christ as being directed toward anything but victory. In Matthew 6:31f, Jesus taught that seekers of his kingdom should not despair about what they would eat, or drink, or wear for these things will be provided. In Matthew 10:19f, Jesus assures his followers that when they are called into account by enemies of the kingdom, there is no need to worry about what to say, "for it will be given to you." In Mark 9:23, Jesus makes this startling statement: "All things are possible to him who believes." Mark 10:27 has it, "All things are possible with God." That just about covers everything, doesn't it? Everything is directed toward victory! Even in dying, the Christian is triumphant for, as we read in John 14:2f, "In my Father's house are many rooms; if it were not so, would I have told you that I go and prepare a place for you? And when I go and prepare a place for you, I will come again and take you to myself, that where I am, you may be also."

Christ invites each of us to be a forerunner, a personification of the Word, a "living example," and victorious over the world!

The Word will not come alive for you until it comes alive in you. It will not come to life in great ideas, great books, or great programs. It comes to life in persons.

May God grant us the grace to allow the Word to become flesh in us!

Lectionary Preaching After Pentecost

Virtually all pastors who make use of the sermons in this book will find their worship life and planning shaped by one of two lectionary series. Most mainline Protestant denominations, along with clergy of the Roman Catholic Church, have now approved — either for provisional or official use — the three-year Common (Consensus) Lectionary. This family of denominations includes United Methodist, Presbyterian, United Church of Christ and Disciples of Christ.

Lutherans and Roman Catholics, while testing the Common Lectionary on a limited basis at present, follow their own three-year cycle of texts. While there are divergences between the Common and Lutheran/Roman Catholic systems, the gospel texts show striking parallels, with few text selections evidencing significant differences. Nearly all the gospel texts included in this book will, therefore, be applicable to worship and preaching planning for clergy following either lectionary.

A significant divergence does occur, however, in the method by which specific gospel texts are assigned to specific calendar days. The Common and Roman Catholic Lectionaries accomplish this by counting backwards from Christ the King (Last Sunday after Pentecost), discarding "extra" texts from the front of the list: Lutherans follow the opposite pattern, counting forward from The Holy Trinity, discarding "extra" texts at the end of the list.

The following index will aid the user of this book in matching the correct text to the correct Sunday during the Pentecost portion of the church year.

(Fixed dates do not pertain to Lutheran Lectionary)

Fixed Date Lectionaries *Common and Roman Catholic*	Lutheran Lectionary *Lutheran*
The Day of Pentecost	The Day of Pentecost
The Holy Trinity	The Holy Trinity
May 29-June 4 — Proper 4, Ordinary Time 9	Pentecost 2
June 5-11 — Proper 5, Ordinary Time 10	Pentecost 3
June 12-18 — Proper 6, Ordinary Time 11	Pentecost 4
June 19-25 — Proper 7, Ordinary Time 12	Pentecost 5
June 26-July 2 — Proper 8, Ordinary Time 13	Pentecost 6

122

July 3-9 — Proper 9, Ordinary Time 14	Pentecost 7
July 10-16 — Proper 10, Ordinary Time 15	Pentecost 8
July 17-23 — Proper 11, Ordinary Time 16	Pentecost 9
July 24-30 — Proper 12, Ordinary Time 17	Pentecost 10
July 31-Aug. 6 — Proper 13, Ordinary Time 18	Pentecost 11
Aug. 7-13 — Proper 14, Ordinary Time 19	Pentecost 12
Aug. 14-20 — Proper 15, Ordinary Time 20	Pentecost 13
Aug. 21-27 — Proper 16, Ordinary Time 21	Pentecost 14
Aug. 28-Sept. 3 — Proper 17, Ordinary Time 22	Pentecost 15
Sept. 4-10 — Proper 18, Ordinary Time 23	Pentecost 16
Sept. 11-17 — Proper 19, Ordinary Time 24	Pentecost 17
Sept. 18-24 — Proper 20, Ordinary Time 25	Pentecost 18
Sept. 25-Oct. 1 — Proper 21, Ordinary Time 26	Pentecost 19
Oct. 2-8 — Proper 22, Ordinary Time 27	Pentecost 20
Oct. 9-15 — Proper 23, Ordinary Time 28	Pentecost 21
Oct. 16-22 — Proper 24, Ordinary Time 29	Pentecost 22
Oct. 23-29 — Proper 25, Ordinary Time 30	Pentecost 23
Oct. 30-Nov. 5 — Proper 26, Ordinary Time 31	Pentecost 24
Nov. 6-12 — Proper 27, Ordinary Time 32	Pentecost 25
Nov. 13-19 — Proper 28, Ordinary Time 33	Pentecost 26 Pentecost 27
Nov. 20-26 — Christ the King	Christ the King

Reformation Day (or last Sunday in October) is October 31 (Common, Lutheran)

All Saints' Day (or first Sunday in November) is November 1 (Common, Lutheran, Roman Catholic)